We need good men to be strong, rise out of shame, and step into their place in God's story. Robert Hotchkin has written a clear action plan for men to fully carry the nature and character of Jesus. I highly recommend *31 Decrees of Blessing for Men* in this season.

—Jamie Galloway, Jamie Galloway Ministries

31 Decrees of Blessing for Men will change your family and your world!

—James W. Goll, God Encounters Ministries, GOLL Ideation LLC

Robert Hotchkin's *31 Decrees of Blessing for Men* is an outstanding devotional for men and will surely bless and encourage all who read it and decree it.

—Dr. Patricia King, author, ministry leader, and television host

Robert Hotchkin is equipping this generation to move into greater power and glory. With *31 Decrees of Blessing for Men*, he has provided a tool to break the shackles off the lives of God's sons and inspire them to reach higher. This book is key for men who want to run into the battle and take down the giant.

—Ryan LeStrange, author, speaker, prophet, and founder of RLM, LeStrange Global, TRIBE, and the iHubs Movement

Here is a spiritually invigorating, meaty, practical, hands-on, doable, rubber-hits-the-road, strengthening resource for God's sons as they navigate through life. It's just plain good!

—Mary Audrey Raycroft, founder of Releasers of Life Equipping Ministry and teaching pastor of Catch the Fire, Toronto

This is a book you need. This is a book *I* need. Walk through this book. No, run through this book! Do these activations and watch God move with power in your life.

—Steve Shultz, founder of Elijah List Ministries

Men need this book! *31 Decrees of Blessing for Men* is a powerful way for guys to get a daily reminder of who they really are and what is available to them in Christ. This book will make a difference in the life of every man who grabs hold of its truth.

—Chris Widener, bestselling author, podcast host of
Fortunes from Speaking

My good friend, Robert Hotchkin, has an amazing revelation concerning the truth that the time has come for the unveiling of the sons of God. The devotions and decrees in this book will help men everywhere step into their identity as true sons of our heavenly Father.

—Dr. Kevin Zadai, founder and president of Warrior Notes and
Warrior Notes School of Ministry

31 DECREES
OF
BLESSING

FOR MEN

ROBERT HOTCHKIN

BroadStreet
PUBLISHING

BroadStreet Publishing® Group, LLC
Savage, Minnesota, USA
BroadStreetPublishing.com

31 Decrees of Blessing for Men

978-1-4245-5993-0 (faux leather)
978-1-4245-5994-7 (e-book)

Stock or custom editions of BroadStreet Publishing titles may be purchased in bulk for educational, business, ministry, fundraising, or sales promotional use. For information, please email info@broadstreetpublishing.com.

Cover and interior by Garborg Design at GarborgDesign.com.

Printed in China
20 21 22 23 24 5 4 3 2 1

DEDICATED TO

Jesus Christ, the Son of God who became the Son of Man so that every son of man could become a son of God.

And to all my Christian brothers and fellow Men on the Frontlines. May you know the certainty of sonship so that you fully receive and fully walk in all the blessings of your heavenly Father who loves you and is so well pleased with you.

CONTENTS

FOREWORD

Men, listen: You are going to be encouraged as you read this book! Loaded with ammunition for your devotional life, these thirty-one decrees of blessing will shake you in a good way. In our culture, countless forces try to discourage the true follower of Jesus, but we must be men who lead lives that are saturated with the culture of heaven. God is about to nudge you closer to his heart, for when you lose yourself in the love of your Father in heaven, you will find your true manhood.

I love to encourage men. I am passionate about showing them the more excellent way of love and bringing them closer to God. I've found that the greatest way of encouraging men is to share the Father's blessings with them. The blessing of God is what every one of us craves; we want to know his blessings over our lives, our families, our health, and our relationships.

A wonderful church in the Boston area is moving forward with God. I'll never forget the men of that church and the privilege I had to bless them. The pastor invited me to speak to the congregation one Sunday morning, but I felt God deeply press upon my heart to speak directly to the men even though many women were present. I shared the Father's blessing over their lives, and immediately I could tell that most of the men needed affirmation and encouragement. It showed on their faces as I spoke.

At the end of the service, I asked all of the men to line up, and I looked each one in the eyes and blessed them. What manly hugs I received that day! Most of the men were weeping as I told them how proud our heavenly Father is of his sons. Some of the men in that room waited up to two hours for me to reach them and share the blessing of a father over them.

I will never forget that meeting and how it impacted the men. The women in the room could see what was taking place, and they, too, were visibly moved. Guys, I know what you want most in life: it's the Father's blessing!

Blessings are a theme throughout the Bible. From the very beginning, we see how much God wants to bless us. Genesis alone contains the words *bless* and *blessing* more than eighty times! He even blessed birds and fish. If God has blessed the fish and birds, imagine how much more blessed you are! God has chosen you to bless you. He wanted you to be his. He wanted a friend and a partner. He wanted someone to walk with and share himself with. You are that one. He chose you because he wanted you. You belong to God—not to your company, your church, or your wallet. You belong to the One who chose you and died for you: "You are among the chosen ones who received the call to belong to Jesus, the Anointed One" (Romans 1:6 TPT).

Men, the wealth of the glory of God's inheritance is in you! In fact, you are the hidden treasure in this world. Man of God, he chose you because you are a treasure that contains the goodness and glory of Jesus Christ. You are his divine poetry. God has chosen you to demonstrate a unique message to the world that only you can present. Your life, your unique gifts, and your passion for God bring a poetic expression of God's love to the world. How does it feel to be the lyrics of God's love on two legs? God has blessed you, and he will use you for his glory as you put him first.

I've read many books written to encourage men, but Robert Hotchkin has written what I believe is the best devotional book a guy could read. It will charge you up and motivate you to change the world around you. With God's blessing on your life, nothing is impossible! You will feel like Robert has written this amazing book just for you. The chapter headings alone got me excited, and the decrees of blessing will linger over your life long after you've finished reading them. This excellent book joins the power of making a decree and the power of a blessing. Robert has done a masterful job of presenting God's heart for men.

Get ready for some life-changing truths to wash over you! Starting today, be determined to see yourself as blessed, and allow these thirty-one decrees to transform your life. Be blessed, my friend!

Brian Simmons

The Passion Translation Project

THE TRUTH ABOUT MEN

Creation waits eagerly for the revealing of the sons of God.
ROMANS 8:19

Popular culture has been lying to us about men for quite some time.

Real men are not lone-wolf lotharios who need nothing except another notch on their bedposts.

Dads are not sitcom simpletons who offer little to their families other than being the easy butt of every joke.

Husbands are not clueless buffoons who make a mess of everything.

Masculinity is not toxic.

In other words, to put it really simply: Men are not "the problem." Just the opposite. We are actually a big part of the divine solution for every problem the world is facing.

When God created humanity in his image, he created us male and female. Then he set us in place as his dominion stewards on the earth to co-labor with him as his divine representatives over all creation (Genesis 1:26–28). This means that the fullest and most potent representation ("re-presentation") of God is when male and female, women and men, choose to walk in all God has blessed us with and called us to.

So yes, men are absolutely necessary. Masculinity is important. We always have been—and always will be—a part of God's plan. We should never ignore, deny, dumb-down, or neuter that.

We need men. We need good, powerful, righteous men. Men who are willing to serve. Men who are willing to lead. Men of faith and men of integrity. Men who embrace their power and potential through restored relationships with their heavenly Father. Men who arise as the heroes, warriors, champions, fathers, husbands, brothers, and friends that God created them to be. All while respecting, supporting, and making places for women who are also a key part of God's divine plan.

All of creation is crying out for these "sons of God" to be revealed (Romans 8:19). It is time that we add our voices to this chorus and cry out for them as well. We can do that through the power of scriptural decrees.

The Power of Decrees

God's Word is amazing. It is living, active, and full of power (Hebrews 4:12). It never returns void, and it accomplishes all that God sent it to do (Isaiah 55:11). God's Word is eternally true, never expires, and will never fade away (40:8). It is certain, potent, and full of promises for every one of us, all the time.

When we decree God's Word in faith it establishes his truth in our lives and on the earth (Job 22:28). Mighty angels are released to obediently perform his Word (Psalm 103:20). According to Romans 4:17, if there is a truth we see in God's Word that is not yet fully manifested in our lives, we can decree that truth with the expectation that it will come forth.

There is power in this book that you hold in your hands—the power of decrees!

As you make these decrees and declare these blessings in faith, you are creating a framework in the spirit that heaven will pour into, bringing forth greater and greater manifestation of God's truth and promises. You are agreeing with what God has done and won in the eternal realm so that it may be established in the temporal realm. You are co-laboring with God the Creator and operating as a dominion steward over the creation of your life. You are helping to bring heaven to earth.

Hebrews 11:3 makes it clear that the entire universe was framed and established by the Word of God and that things in the natural are actually formed by things of the spirit. For example, when the Lord spoke forth the words "Let there be light," there was light (Genesis 1:3). That wasn't a one-time event. As we see in Isaiah 55:11, the Word of God *always* produces fruit. It accomplishes *everything* God sends it forth to do, and it *will* prosper. Always.

You can put that kind of power to work in your life every day. That's what this book is for.

Daily Decrees for Year-Round Blessing

31 Decrees of Blessing for Men puts the power of God's Word in your hands and in your mouth so that you can speak the truth of his kingdom into your life.

There is a devotion, decree, and activation for every day of the month.

Each devotion focuses on an empowering scripture that reveals a key blessing God has for his sons. The devotion will build up your faith and expectancy that this blessing is real and that it is for you.

After each devotion, there is a series of decrees. As you speak forth these spiritual truths, you are establishing them in your life. These words will not return void. They will accomplish all God sends them to do. They will produce fruit.

Scriptural references follow each day's decrees. These references make it simple for you to find the source passages for the decrees. Look them up in your Bible. Read them over and over. Focus and meditate on them. Allow them to renew your mind. Allow them to build and multiply the substance of your faith. Allow them to root you and ground you in the certainty of God's blessing for you. Afterward, go back and proclaim the decrees again with an even greater substance of faith and hope-filled expectation.

Every day also contains an activation. These activations provide you with ideas on how you can put feet to your faith and step into the reality of the spiritual realm you have established by receiving, believing, and decreeing the Word of God. They give you something that you can do to activate the blessing in your life.

What the World Needs Now

The apostle Paul planted a church in the Greek city of Corinth during his second missionary journey. After his departure, all sorts of problems began to pop up. Rebellion. Dishonor and disrespect. Immorality. False theologies. Jealousy. Competition. And more. Paul wrote a letter to the church in Corinth to help them deal with the issues in a godly, effective way. Near the end of his letter, he summed up all of his input and insights with the following counsel: "Be on the alert, stand firm in the faith, *act like men*, be strong" (1 Corinthians 16:13).

What was true in Paul's day is still true today. It has been true since day six of creation when God made us in his image—male and female—and placed us on the earth as his dominion stewards (Genesis 1:26–28). Men are part of the plan. Men are part of the solution. Men are necessary. When godly men righteously inhabit their place in every sphere of influence, they help solve problems, and every part of society improves.

Right now, perhaps more than ever, the world needs good, strong, faith-filled, Christian men. One of the simplest and most powerful ways we, as Christian men, can allow God to strengthen us is by knowing and declaring his Word.

Men, we can use the daily devotionals, decrees, and activations in this book to strengthen ourselves—to become the husbands, fathers, sons, brothers, friends, leaders, servants, problem-solvers, and blessings our heavenly Father created us to be.

Wives can use them to strengthen their husbands.

Parents can use them to strengthen their sons.

Pastors can use them to strengthen the men under their spiritual covering, and congregations can use them to strengthen their male pastors.

Employers can use them to strengthen their male employees, and workers can use them to strengthen their male bosses.

My prayer for you as you pick up and use *31 Decrees of Blessing for Men* is that each and every day you will encounter the love and encouragement of your heavenly Father. I pray that this book will remind you of the beloved son that you are and the power you have in Christ to not only be blessed but to be a blessing.

The world needs good, strong Christian men in this hour. The world needs you.

You matter. You are important. You have a key role to play for the kingdom on the earth. So believe, receive, declare, and be blessed!

Expect great things!

Robert Hotchkin
Men on the Frontlines
RobertHotchkin.com
MenontheFrontlines.com

BLESSED WITH THE CERTAINTY OF SONSHIP

"You are My beloved Son, in You I am well-pleased."

MARK 1:11

What the Father says to the Son in Mark 1:11 is powerful. What really blows me away, however, is when he says it. This declaration of complete love and total acceptance comes at the very beginning of Jesus's earthly ministry, before he has done anything.

At this point Jesus has not saved or healed anyone. He has not worked any miracles or fed a single person, let alone a multitude. He hasn't cleansed a leper. He hasn't raised the dead. He hasn't cast out a single demon or overcome a single temptation. He hasn't even preached a message yet. He hasn't put the reality of his Father and his kingdom on display in any way to anyone, and he certainly has not yet gone to the cross and fulfilled his purpose and destiny on the earth. At this point, the Son hasn't done a thing. Yet the heavens are open. The Holy Spirit pours out. And the Father holds nothing back.

This announcement dramatically puts on display for all to see that the kingdom of God on the earth is not based on performance; it is based on relationship. The Father did not love and accept the

Son because he did good—he hadn't done anything yet. The Father loved and accepted the Son because the Father is good.

The heavens were opened and the Holy Spirit poured out not because of what the Son accomplished *for* the Father but because of who the Son was *to* the Father. This is the message of Mark 1:11. It is God declaring, "All that I am and all that I have is all for you all the time for no other reason than you are My Son!"

This is how God sent Jesus out into the world: with a declaration of total love and complete acceptance simply because of relationship.

I am sure you can understand that the Father felt this way about Jesus. What I want you to understand today is that he also very much feels this way about you.

Romans 8:29 makes it clear that one of the reasons Jesus came to the earth was so that he would be the firstborn of *many* sons. You are now one of those sons, and the Father feels about you exactly as he felt about Jesus (John 17:23).

With that in mind, you can see that Mark 1:11 is not only how God sent the Son out into his calling. It is how God sends out every son (John 20:21), including you.

Every day and in every set of circumstances, you can be certain of one thing above all else—you are a son. With that certainty of sonship comes the deep knowing that your heavenly Father loves you, is well pleased with you, and holds nothing back from you. Ever.

On your good days.

On your bad days.

Every day.

All the time.

All of his kingdom is for you.

When you are doing great, you can be certain that you are loved, accepted, and that your heavenly Father is well pleased with you, but you can also be just as certain on those days when you are wrestling or when you have blown it.

Never again do you need to fear or doubt. Never again do you need to question. For all of your days, from this moment forward, you can be certain that all of your Father's blessings, provision, protection, and power are available to you for no other reason than because you are his son.

DECREES

I DECREE THAT:

1. I am a son of God.
2. On my good days, I am his son.
3. On my bad days, I am his son.
4. My heavenly Father loves me completely and accepts me totally.
5. He is well pleased with me.
6. I do not need to perform for love and acceptance.
7. I do not need to work for relationship with my heavenly Father.
8. He is always there for me.
9. All of his kingdom and all of his blessings are always available to me.
10. God sends me out every day and into every situation with the safety and security of the certainty of sonship.

Decrees based on the following Scriptures: Mark 1:11; Romans 8:29, 38–39; John 17:23; Ephesians 1:3; 2 Peter 1:3

ACTIVATION

Think of a situation where you feel disqualified from a blessing of God because you handled things poorly, made a bad decision, or just flat out blew it. Now bring to mind the greater truth that you walk in the certainty of sonship and that all of God's love, approval, provision, and blessings are yours simply because you are in relationship with him. Shake off any residual guilt, shame, fear, or condemnation. Declare that you are a son. Claim that blessing. Declare it is yours because you are his.

Day Two

Blessed with Power

When he had called unto him his twelve disciples,
he gave them power.
Matthew 10:1 KJV

I spend a lot of time on airplanes. Some weeks, the only free time that I seem to have is when I'm at thirty-five thousand feet. This is often when I catch up on emails, get some writing done, or have the chance for impromptu quiet time with the Lord.

A few years ago on a flight back from the East Coast, I had just put on my headphones, cued up some worship music, and was about to enter in with the Lord when we hit some serious turbulence. The pilot came on the intercom and announced that the flight attendants needed to suspend the beverage service and strap in because we were in for a bumpy ride for the next twenty minutes until we cleared some rough air.

I like to fly, but I do not like severe turbulence. As the shaking began to increase, I spoke to the Lord and told him, *Lord, I was really looking forward to some quiet time with you. Could you please do something about all the bumping and shaking?*

He spoke a gentle and encouraging response to my heart: *You do it.*

In an instant, he brought to mind the story of when he stood in the boat and spoke to the storm telling the wind and the waves to be still (Mark 4:39). He reminded me that as a believer, I have received the call to do the works that he did (John 14:12). If Jesus is the same yesterday, today, and forever (Hebrews 13:8) and he works with us everywhere we go (Mark 16:20), then it made sense to me that what worked at sea level *for* him should work at cruising altitude *with* him.

At the leading of the Holy Spirit, I began to pray. I quietly spoke to the storm of the air, commanding the waves of wind that were buffeting the plane to "Be still!" Within a moment, the rough air smoothed. A few seconds later, the pilot came back on the intercom, and with a surprised voice, he announced that the turbulence had suddenly disappeared. He let the flight attendants know it was now safe to get up and resume the beverage service. Praise the Lord!

That began a journey with the Holy Spirit of learning to rise up in the power we receive as sons of the King to do the works that Jesus did.

We are so much more powerful than we realize.

We can speak to storms and tell them to be still.

We can heal the sick.

We can cleanse the lepers.

We can cast out demons.

We can raise the dead.

We can love the difficult.

We can move in peace, joy, compassion, kindness, and patience when the rest of the world is panicking, anxious, irritated, and afraid.

We can do the works that Jesus did, and even greater works because the very same power that raised Jesus from the dead dwells in us—dwells in *you* (Acts 1:8)!

Think about that. The *very same* power that helped Jesus defeat every work of the enemy and even overcome death itself is in you. Jesus has given it to you just like he gave it to his other disciples. He wants to help mentor you in how to use that power so that you can walk in victory and bring glory to his name.

Holy Spirit power! Miracle-working power! Every-battle-winning power! It's yours. You have it all the time—in your relationships, at your workplace, in your community, in your finances, in your health, in your prayers, and in your devotional times. This power has blessed you in every situation and circumstance you will ever face.

You are powerful!

DECREES

I DECREE THAT:

1. I am a disciple of Jesus Christ.
2. He has filled me with his Holy Spirit and with power.
3. The very same power that raised Jesus from the dead dwells within me.
4. I will never face a situation that Christ has not empowered me to overcome and see victory.
5. I have the power to heal the sick, cleanse the lepers, cast out demons, and raise the dead.
6. I have the power to speak to any "storm" that is creating any kind of "turbulence" in my life and command it to be still.
7. I have the power to speak to "any mountains" that are blocking or hindering my way, and they shall be removed.
8. He has given me the power to make wealth and live in abundance.
9. In him, I have the power to work notable and remarkable miracles and put the reality of his kingdom on display wherever I go.
10. I can do all things through Christ who has blessed me with power.

Decrees based on the following Scriptures: Matthew 10:1; Acts 10:38; Romans 8:11; Matthew 10:8; Mark 4:39; Mark 11:23; Deuteronomy 8:18; Acts 19:11; Philippians 4:13

ACTIVATION

Acts 1:8 promises that the Holy Spirit will come upon you and that you will receive power. Ask him to give you a fresh filling of power and a renewed revelation that there is nothing of the enemy—not even death itself—that can stand against the power of God that you bring to every situation you face.

_____

_____

_____

_____

_____

_____

_____

_____

_____

_____

_____

Day Three

Blessed with Authority

*"Behold, I have given you authority to tread on serpents
and scorpions, and over all the power of the enemy,
and nothing will injure you."*

Luke 10:19

Yesterday, we looked at how God has blessed you with power. Today we are going to look at how God has also blessed you with authority. Power is the capability to do something. Authority is the official backing that gives you permission to do it.

When I was seventeen, I couldn't vote in a presidential election in my country. It's not because I wasn't capable of getting to a voting booth and filling out a ballot. It's rather that in my country you're not legally allowed to vote until you are eighteen.

I had the ability to vote when I was seventeen, but if I had done so, ballot counters would have ignored my ballot because I did not have legal permission to vote. I had the power but not the authority.

It works similarly in the kingdom. Think of the sons of Sceva in Acts 19:13–16. These seven guys had heard about the miracle power that God had given the apostle Paul (Acts 19:11–12), so they decided to have a go at it for themselves. They tried using the name of Jesus to cast out an evil spirit from a man. Their efforts did not affect the spirit in the least. It replied to them by saying, "I know Jesus, and I know Paul. But who are you?" The evil spirit recognized the power of the name of Jesus, but it also knew that the seven sons of Sceva, unlike Paul, did not have the authority to use that power. As a result, the demon ignored their command and attacked them so violently that they had to flee, screaming and afraid.

You don't have to be concerned about that.

You not only have the power to cast out demons—and to heal the sick and raise the dead and all the other things we looked at yesterday—but you also have the authority to do it. It says so right there in Luke 10:19. You have nothing to fear in the natural. You have nothing to fear in the spirit. You can stand against any manifestation of the enemy, and nothing will injure you because God has given you the power and the authority.

This has been God's plan since day six of creation. He has always wanted to have a people in relationship with him who rule and reign on the earth by operating in his power as his authorized dominion stewards (Genesis 1:26–28). When you accepted Jesus as your Lord and Savior, you stepped right back into this original plan. You stepped right back into relationship with the Lord. In that relationship, you received power to move in the miraculous as well as the permission, covering, and protection to do so.

Because God has blessed you with authority, you never need to be afraid of the enemy. When you really understand this, however, the enemy will need to be very afraid of you.

DECREES

I Decree That:

1. God has blessed me to operate as a dominion steward on the earth.
2. I am authorized to move in Holy Spirit power to the glory of Jesus Christ.
3. I have authority over all the power of the enemy.
4. Nothing will injure me.
5. Nothing in the natural.
6. Nothing in the spirit.
7. Christ covers and protects me.
8. Because of the kingdom authority I walk in, the enemy must bow everywhere I go. Sickness must bow, lack must bow, and oppression must bow.
9. Nothing of the enemy can stand in my life.
10. Nothing of the enemy can stand against me as I stand in the kingdom authority God has blessed me with.

Decrees based on the following Scriptures: Genesis 1:26–28; Luke 10:19; Isaiah 54:17

ACTIVATION

When you pray and nothing *seems* to happen, the enemy will try to lie to you and tell you that your prayers are not working. He wants to convince you that he does not need to heed your decrees. He wants you to feel discouraged or frustrated and give up. Remember, you not only have the ability to send forth God's Word, which never returns void (Isaiah 55:11), but you also have authority over the power of the enemy. Stand in that authority, specifically in any area where the enemy seems to be resisting you. Declare that all of heaven covers, protects, empowers, and backs you up every time you make your decrees and declarations. Exercise your Luke 10:19 authority over all the power of the enemy!

_____

_____

_____

_____

_____

_____

_____

_____

BLESSED WITH FAVOR

*"I have known you by name,
and you have also found favor in My sight."*

EXODUS 33:12

Favor is amazing. Favor is incredible. Favor is a force. It opens doors, it makes connections, it attracts blessings, and it provides advantages.

Being blessed with favor is like being magnetized to attract blessing, opportunity, and good things.

When you are walking in the favor of God, good things just seem to happen all the time, everywhere you go. You won't be able to explain it, but you won't need to. You are simply enjoying the favor of God.

Years ago, when I was still fairly new in ministry, I was invited to be part of a prophetic roundtable dinner discussion sponsored by a major publisher at an event I was attending. There were many ministers there, all of whom were much better known than I was. Still, the senior editorial member of the publisher's staff chose to sit next to me. The editor also spent the entire evening talking with me. At the end of the night, the editor asked me to publish a book with them based on some of the revelation I had shared during our meal.

When a friend found out I was getting ready to sign a book deal with the publisher, she told me that she had tried to submit some ideas to that same publishing house years prior but had been told she needed to have a literary agent before the publisher would even consider her proposal.

I didn't have an agent. I wasn't a headline speaker back then. I didn't even have a name most people would have heard of. At that point, I also didn't have a track record of big book sales.

What I had, though, was favor.

You have it too. Once you are aware that God has blessed you with favor, you will begin to expect and draw good things to you.

Favor is when someone holds you in high regard, approves of you, gives you privileges and special treatment, showers you with blessings you have neither earned nor merited, and makes you the beneficiary of goodwill, benefits, and gifts. Doesn't that sound like how God thinks of you and what he has done for you?

When you were still given over to darkness, Jesus gave his life for you. When you were in love with the wicked ways of the world, he so loved you that he chose to die for your sins so that you might have eternal life. Now that's favor! Blessedly, that's only the beginning. The amazing favor that you have with God that brought you into a saving knowledge of Christ and all the bounty and blessings of his kingdom can actually increase each and every day (Luke 2:52).

Scripture promises that because you are in Christ, the Lord surrounds you with his favor as a shield (Psalm 5:12). That means favor not only creates opportunities for you and draws blessings to you, but it also defends you against your enemies. Just like in Genesis 26:28 when Isaac's enemies saw that the Lord was with him, and they didn't want to oppose him anymore. Now they wanted to be his allies, and they gave him a prime piece of territory to prove it.

God loves you. He thinks you are amazing. He gave his life for you. You are special to him, the very apple of his eye. Of course he has blessed you with favor!

DECREES

I Decree That:

1. God has blessed and highly favored me.
2. Every day I increase in favor with God and with man.
3. Doors open for me.
4. Opportunities come to me.
5. Blessings flow to me.
6. Favor surrounds me like a shield. I am covered, protected, and preferred in every situation I find myself and with everyone I meet.
7. People who were once against me are now for me.
8. The favor of God rests upon me and blesses everything I put my hand to. All of my work is blessed.
9. Everyone who meets me holds me in high regard. Kingdom connections and divine appointments are a daily occurrence in my life.
10. Because the divine favor of God has blessed me, I expect and draw good things to me.

Decrees based on the following Scriptures: Luke 1:28; 2:52; Psalm 5:12; Genesis 26:28; Psalm 90:17; Psalm 23:6

ACTIVATION

God loves you. He loves you so much that he gave his Son for you. That's the truth of how divinely favored you are! Now think of an area of your life where it doesn't look or feel like you're favored. Maybe it's your career. Maybe it's your finances. Maybe it's a relationship. Instead of believing the report of your past experiences, begin to declare the favor of the Lord in that specific area. Every day, by faith, receive the favor of the Lord in that area until you are certain it is bathed in divine advantage and until you expect good results and blessings to come forth.

_____

_____

_____

_____

_____

_____

_____

_____

_____

_____

DAY FIVE

BLESSED WITH THE PRESENCE OF GOD

"And be sure of this: I am with you always."
MATTHEW 28:20 NLT

The presence of God is a powerful thing. During the Old Testament when God was with his people in war, they won every battle. When God was among the people in the New Testament, the sick were healed, the dead were raised, demons were cast out, and miracles were a regular occurrence.

Moses knew what it meant to have the presence of God with him. He didn't want to do anything without it. He actually told the Lord that there was no point to go on if God himself did not go with him (Exodus 33:15–16). Not even an angelic escort was good enough. He wanted *God* with him.

This was pleasing to the Lord. It so touched his heart that he called Moses his friend, assured Moses that he would "personally go" with him, and that because of God's presence, Moses would have rest and all would be well for him (vv. 14–17 NLT).

Unlike Moses, there is no need for you to cry out for the presence of the Lord. You already have it. God's Word assures you of it. God promises you this in Matthew 28:20 when he tells you that he will be with you always.

Always!

How amazing is that? At all times and in all situations, you can be certain that God is with you.

God made you to walk with him on the earth, to be surrounded by the reality of who he is, to enjoy the fullness of his goodness, and to see heaven touch earth through you because of his presence in you and all around you. You're designed for it. It is your "original" state.

We see evidence of this initial intent in the Garden of Eden when the Lord came to walk with Adam each evening (Genesis 3:8). In Christ, you are restored to this. That's the promise of the Messiah, Jesus Immanuel (Isaiah 7:14; Matthew 1:22–23). Jesus's name literally tells us that he is the Lord who brings salvation. The promise of that salvation is "Immanuel" which means "God with us." Jesus came to restore you to relationship with your heavenly Father and know and enjoy his presence—always. Immanuel does not mean "God occasionally with you" or "God might be with you." No. It means "God *is* with you."

Over the years, I have had many powerful experiences of the presence of the Lord. Seeing him, feeling him, sensing the reality of his right-there-ness. I am deeply grateful for every one of those encounters. However, what is most wonderful and amazing to me about God is that we can be certain of his presence at all times. When we feel it and sense it and just as much when we don't.

God is not more "present" during tangible encounters, visions, and visitations when we sense or see him. We are simply more aware of his presence at those times. They are beautiful reminders of what is always true for each and every one of us all the time. God *is* with us!

You have been blessed with the presence of God. You can be sure of it. You can also expect all the blessings and benefits of living in his presence.

DECREES

I DECREE THAT:

1. God is with me.
2. Every moment of every day, I walk with the Lord, and he walks with me.
3. I am always in his presence, and he is always present.
4. The Lord never leaves me, he never forsakes me, and he never fails me.
5. In whatever is before me, I can go forth in strength, expecting a good outcome because the Lord, my God, is with me.
6. I never need to be afraid because the Lord is with me.
7. The presence of God surrounds me, now and forever.
8. The presence of God fills me.
9. I am overflowing with his presence.
10. I am blessed with the presence of the Lord always, when I feel it and when I don't. I am always with him because he is always with me.

Decrees based on the following Scriptures: Psalm 118:6; Matthew 28:20; Joshua 1:9; Judges 6:12, 14; Psalm 23:4; Psalm 125:2; Ephesians 3:19; John 7:38

ACTIVATION

God is with you. When you feel him and when you don't. When you are aware of him and when you aren't. The reality of his presence does not change or increase. Your level of awareness of his presence, however, does. The more you agree with the truth of his presence, the more he will establish the reality of it in your life. Take time every day to agree with the truth that God is with you. Set a timer on your phone, and for that time, focus on the truth and reality that God *is* with you. Thank him for his presence. Thank him that he is there. Thank him that he never leaves you. Declare during those times when you do not feel or sense his presence that you are still certain that he is there because he promises it in his Word. You may not feel or sense any increase of his tangible presence in the moment, but by agreeing with eternal truth over and over again, you are establishing a realm of the reality of his presence in your life.

_____

_____

_____

_____

_____

_____

_____

BLESSED WITH THE ABILITY TO CHANGE ATMOSPHERES

God created man in His own image . . . and God said to them,
"Be fruitful and multiply, and fill the earth, and subdue it;
and rule."

GENESIS 1:27–28

For six years, the main focus of my ministry was leading our Operation Extreme Love Thailand trips into Pattaya. I mentored teams from all over the world on how to bring the extreme love of Jesus into extreme situations. Every day we saw wonderful things happen—salvations, healings, deliverances, miracles. It was amazing. Sometimes there were people lined up in the streets waiting for prayer and ministry because they were so hungry for a touch from God.

Then, through an angelic encounter, the Lord called me to Europe, specifically a key region of Eastern Europe. Surprisingly, it was substantially different from the atmosphere I had experienced in Thailand.

On my first trip into Eastern Europe, no one would talk to me on the streets. If I said hello, people completely ignored me and hurried away from me. When I tried to talk to waiters, waitresses, or people in shops, it was the same. No one wanted to talk. No one was willing to let me pray for them. No one wanted to interact or connect. Everyone was so guarded and shut off. They just wanted to be left alone.

I tried to get locals to go on outreach with me, but they told me that there was no point. They said only drunks or crazy people talk to strangers on the street or in shops, so there was no way people would be willing to stop for a conversation. On top of this cultural roadblock, there was also a tangible spiritual atmosphere of heaviness and oppression hanging over the region from decades of Soviet occupation and domination.

Still, the Lord had called me there, so I knew he must have a plan. When I asked what it was, he invited me to launch a "smile ministry." He asked me to go out onto the streets, into the shops, parks, and public places and simply walk and pray, and whenever I could catch someone's eye, even if only for a second, smile at them—a warm, kind, caring smile.

So that's what I did. Every day. Sometimes for hours at a time. I also shared the vision of the "smile ministry" in every church where I preached and ministered, inviting others to join me in this "outreach" as they went about their days.

It was that simple. Smile. And it worked.

Over time, the entire atmosphere of the city changed, from dark and dour to light and joyful and from those first outings when people moved away from me as quickly as they could to us having teams out on the streets and in the parks ministering to people. And yes, just like in Thailand, there were even times when folks were lined up so that we could pray for them, prophesy over them, and encourage them.

Of course it worked. It had to because God has blessed us with the ability to change atmospheres. It's part of our role as dominion stewards on the earth who care for and cultivate creation. It's right there in Genesis 1.

The Bible starts with a display of divine atmosphere changing. God shifts things from darkness to light. From chaos to order. From void to filled with life. Right after all that, he makes us in his image and puts us in place to tend to his creation. And look at what he says when he does it: be "fruitful and multiply," and this action will "fill the earth." God is not being redundant when he tells us to be both "fruitful" and to "multiply." He is not simply repeating himself and saying the same thing twice. He is giving us a key to operating on the earth as his dominion stewards. He is announcing that we can "multiply" the reality of his kingdom on the earth by being "fruitful," or by being full of fruit. His Fruit. The fruit of the Holy Spirit. Galatians 5:22–23 tells us what this fruit is: "the fruit of the Spirit is love, joy, peace, patience, kindness, goodness, faithfulness, gentleness, and self-control."

Look at those atmosphere changers! Love. Joy. Peace. Patience. Kindness. Goodness. Faithfulness. Gentleness. Perhaps the most important one is there at the end: self-control.

As dominion stewards, it is key that we realize that the first realm we must watch over is ourselves. If we watch over our moods, emotions, and words, we can affect and change whole atmospheres. It's easy to give into a prevailing mood of negativity, fear, or doubt. However, it's powerful to choose to intentionally move in an opposite spirit of love, kindness, hope, faith, and positivity. Fortunately, you can do it because, as a son of God, you have been blessed with the ability to change atmospheres.

All through the Gospels, we see Jesus model this for us as well. Where there was sickness, death, lack, or unbelief, he brought forth health and life and abundance and faith. In other words, he changed atmospheres, and he told us to do the same. This is how he put it in Matthew 10:7–8: "'And as you go, preach, saying, "The kingdom of heaven is at hand.". . . Freely you received, freely give.'"

He makes it quite clear. Because we have received the kingdom from him, we can announce wherever we are that the kingdom is now present. It doesn't matter how long or how severely things have not lined up with the kingdom—now they will.

This, of course, applies to dealing with sickness, oppression, death, and even demonic possession. Truly, it applies to any "atmosphere" that is not on earth as it is in heaven. If there is fear or depression or anxiety or irritation or impatience or selfishness or jealousy or cruelty or unrighteousness, you have the power to change it. In a conversation. A room. A workplace. A family. Even a city or nation. God has blessed you with the ability to change atmospheres wherever you are.

DECREES

I Decree That:

1. I am a dominion steward on the earth.
2. I have a positive influence everywhere I go and on everyone I meet.
3. The fruits and power of the Holy Spirit fill me, and I fill the earth with his presence and personality.
4. Wherever I go, darkness becomes light, and the atmosphere shifts on earth as it is in heaven.
5. Greater is he that is in me than anything that is in the earth.
6. Every negative, dark, fear-filled, oppressed atmosphere must bow to the power and personality of Christ within me.
7. I am overflowing with love, joy, peace, patience, kindness, goodness, faithfulness, and gentleness.
8. I choose to operate in self-control by the power of the Holy Spirit and to the glory of God.
9. I watch over my words, my thoughts, and my emotions so that I can intentionally have a positive influence everywhere I am.
10. I do not let my feelings rule me, but instead, I steward my feelings. I choose to move in love, peace, joy, kindness, patience, and the very character and nature of Christ within me because everywhere I go, I am blessed to change atmospheres for the better.

Decrees based on the following Scriptures: Genesis 1:26–28; Matthew 5:14; Galatians 5:22–23; Genesis 1:3; 1 John 4:4; Proverbs 18:20–21

ACTIVATION

The next time you find yourself in a negative atmosphere, be intentional about changing it. If you are around coworkers who are saying negative and dishonoring things about the boss, think of one truly good thing about that person and mention it. If you are around people who are murmuring and complaining, begin to speak out positive things. If you are in a slow line at a store and everyone else is being impatient and irritated, choose to not give into the temptation to also be annoyed, and instead, be thankful and encouraging when it is your turn to check out. Whatever the "dark" atmosphere is, remember that in Christ you are able to move in the opposite spirit of the darkness and release light to change the atmosphere.

Blessed with Rest

"I will give you rest—everything will be fine for you."

Exodus 33:14 NLT

In Christ, there is no need to wait for a day of Sabbath to enter into rest. Christ is our Sabbath. We can always rest in him and his finished work no matter what is going on.

Ministry life is very full and busy with all the travel, events, meetings, media, preaching, and prophesying, and that's just the public part of ministry. There is way more that goes on behind the scenes. It can be a lot. I believe that's why early on in my ministry life God taught me the importance of rest.

At the end of my second year of traveling and preaching, the Lord invited me to take some time out for a prayer retreat. He had shown me many things that he had planned for me in the coming year, so I thought some prayer time was a great idea.

My plan was to head to a remote place up in the mountains and spend ten focused days seeking the Lord and contending for the fulfillment of all he had shown me. I was going to rise early every morning, pray in tongues for eight hours a day, declare the Word of the Lord over the coming year, push back against any possible resistance of the enemy, war, birth, and get things done!

The first morning, the alarm did not go off. I ended up sleeping past ten in the morning. When I saw the clock, I was shocked. I never sleep in like that. Then I felt guilty. I had carved out this prayer time to get things done, not to lie around. I decided I would pray in tongues for two extra hours that day to make up for it. The next thing I knew, I was waking up again. I had fallen back to sleep. I had slept half the day away!

I rebuked laziness. I bound the spirit of sloth. I told sluggishness, indolence, and lethargy to get thee behind me. Still, I was having trouble getting out of bed.

I cried out to the Lord, asking him to reveal what was going on so I would know how to deal with it. He showed me, so clearly, that there was an angel on each side of me, pressing my shoulders to the bed. *He* was not letting me up!

He spoke to my heart and said, *Son, I want to teach you how to enter my rest.*

But I have things I need to do, I thought.

Exactly, was his response, *but you will get more done, and much more easily, if you learn how to do it all from the place of rest.*

The learning began, as it so often does, with him taking me into his Word. Genesis 2:2 says, "By the seventh day God completed His work which He had done, and He rested on the seventh day from all His work which He had done." As I read that passage, the Lord whispered to my heart, *Do you see why I rested on the seventh day?*

I thought, *Well, it is right there. Twice. Because you were finished.*

Exactly. It is the same for you. When you realize that it is finished, you enter into rest.

With that, John 19:30 came into my mind. That's where Jesus on the cross declares, "It is finished!" He wasn't just referring to his time on the earth being finished or his suffering on our behalf. He was referring to his assignment. He was saying that he had dealt with every work of the enemy and every bit of the curse (1 John 3:8). They were finished. It was done.

The key to entering into the rest he has blessed you with is to believe that he has already taken care of everything. It's not that you will never have anything to do. As a man, you are made to get things done. When God brought forth Adam, he gave man assignments—be fruitful, multiply, fill the earth, and rule

(Genesis 1:26–28). There was work to be done but in rest, not in toil. Toil came after the fall.

Jesus has set you free from the curse and from toil. He has taken care of everything. So now, you can enter into his rest and work *from* victory, not for victory. *From* completion, not for completion. No striving necessary. No worry or anxiety needed.

Whatever you are facing, whatever you are going through, anything you've been wrestling with, right now, turn it all over to the Lord. He has taken care of it. He has taken care of everything. Whatever it is, it is finished.

As you choose to believe that, you will enter into the blessing of his rest and all will be well for you!

DECREES

I DECREE THAT:

1. The Lord gives me rest. He blesses me. All is well for me.
2. I turn every care, concern, and worry over to the Lord.
3. It is well with my soul.
4. I am at rest in the Lord.
5. My heart and my mind are at peace.
6. The Lord is my refuge, my strength, and my safe place.
7. I do not fear, and I will not be anxious in any way about anything.
8. Thank you, Lord, that you help me enter into your rest.
9. Thank you, Lord, that you lead me into a quiet peaceful place within myself where I remember that you have already taken care of all that I am facing.
10. Thank you, Lord, that you have blessed me with rest and that you give me the grace to enter your rest at every moment.

Decrees based on the following Scriptures: Exodus 33:14; Psalm 55:22; 1 Peter 5:7; Psalm 46:1–2; Psalm 23:1–3

ACTIVATION

Think of an area of your life where you're not currently at rest. An area where you're striving, anxious, or even filled with fear. Now choose to believe that Jesus has dealt with the situation you are facing. That it is finished. If it's a prodigal you're worried about, remember that you have called upon the name of the Lord, you're saved, and your household shall be as well (Acts 16:31). If it's a financial situation, remember that the Lord will meet all your needs according to his riches in glory in Christ Jesus (Philippians 4:19). Whatever it is, know that Jesus has finished the work in that area so that you can enter his rest. Now, bring that area back to mind. With the assurance of faith, declare that this situation you are facing is finished. Declare that Jesus has dealt with it. Then simply ask him what steps you are to take, while resting in him, to see the victory come forth.

_____

_____

_____

_____

_____

_____

_____

_____

BLESSED WITH GENEROSITY

The harvest of your generosity will grow.
You will be abundantly enriched in every way
as you give generously on every occasion.

2 CORINTHIANS 9:10–11 TPT

So often when we think about divine provision, we tend to focus on the blessing of what God gives to us. Certainly, God pouring out blessings upon us is wonderful. However, if we want to really tap into kingdom enrichment, we need to talk about the blessing of generosity.

God will supply all our needs according to his riches in glory (Philippians 4:19). He has us covered, but he wants us to be more than covered. That's why he has blessed us with generosity. Being a giver, like him (John 3:16), is the key to an ever-increasing harvest. It is the secret to not only being blessed and provided for but also for tapping into the divine realm of abundant enrichment. It says so right there in 2 Corinthians 9:10–11.

Think of it like this: if you are hungry and someone gives you an apple to eat, that meets a need. That's a blessing. If you are blessed with an opportunity to sow an apple seed, the blessing is even greater because that seed will grow an apple tree that is full of apples. Plus, those apples are full of lots more apple seeds, which will grow more trees and, in turn, will bring forth more and more apples and seeds. You end up abundantly enriched with an entire orchard of blessing. All of your needs are more than met along the way, and the harvest of your generosity continues to multiply.

God gives us opportunities to be generous so that we have the chance for blessings beyond anything we can think or imagine.

My good friend Brad Carter is the lead pastor of Calvary Wallace. It is one of the most blessed and thriving churches I have been to anywhere in the world. He and his leadership team have created a kingdom culture that includes generosity as one of their core values. Years ago the Lord gave him an amazing revelation of how powerful it is to embrace the blessing of generosity.

Brad was part of a large conference. One of the other speakers had just delivered a stirring message on generosity. The Lord spoke to Brad and invited him to empty his checking account and sow a radically generous gift. He consulted with his wife. She agreed but did have one question. She asked, "What are we believing for?" Without even thinking, Brad immediately replied, "We are going to be totally debt-free." He didn't know how. He didn't even know why he was so certain that being debt-free was the blessing that would come forth from this opportunity to be generous.

Three days later, Brad got a call from a man who lived about ninety minutes away. He said, "Pastor, I know this is a strange question, but do you mind me asking how much debt you have?" Brad replied, "Sure, we have about $15,000 in debt aside from our home." The man told him, "The Lord spoke to me this morning and told me to write you a check to get you out of debt!" How amazing is God?

Brad is also a man of integrity. He knew he was about to replace his old truck and felt he needed to share this with his divine benefactor. Brad was concerned that if the man came to town and saw they had a new vehicle, he would worry Brad had gone out and spent the blessing on a truck as opposed to actually paying off their debt. When he shared this, the man said, "I'm sorry, Pastor, but I know what God told me. I'm not going to write you a check for $15,000. Instead, I'll send one for $35,000 so you can pay cash for your new vehicle!" Talk about being abundantly enriched and receiving a "harvest of generosity"!

When God meets our needs, it is a blessing. However, he wants us to step into a realm way beyond simply having our needs met. That's why he blesses us with opportunities to be generous. He knows that when we give generously, he gives back even more abundantly!

DECREES

I DECREE THAT:

1. I am a generous giver made in the image of my generous, giving heavenly Father.
2. I give generously of my time, my finances, my patience, and every good thing with which the Lord has blessed me.
3. In every area that I am generous, I grow all the richer.
4. Because I am always generous, I am never in lack, and I am always increasing.
5. The harvest of my generosity is continuously growing.
6. God has abundantly enriched me in every way as I give generously whenever I have the opportunity.
7. As I sow generously, I reap abundantly.
8. The Lord is opening the floodgates of heaven and pouring out blessings I cannot contain.
9. God has generously blessed me, and I generously bless everyone I encounter.
10. The Lord has blessed me with generosity. I look for opportunities to be generous, and I look forward to the abundant harvest of my generosity.

Decrees based on the following Scriptures: Genesis 1:26–28; John 3:16; Matthew 7:11; Proverbs 11:24–25; 2 Corinthians 9:10–11; 2 Corinthians 9:6; Malachi 3:10

ACTIVATION

Look for opportunities to be generous. The next time you are in line at the coffee shop, ask the person in front of you or behind you if you can bless them by paying for their order. When you're at the grocery store, look for someone whose groceries you can buy. Be on the lookout for the chance to be generous with your patience, kindness, love, or encouragement. Ask God to help you see an opportunity to be generous every day. Be sure to call in your "harvest of generosity" along the way!

_____

_____

_____

_____

_____

_____

_____

_____

_____

_____

DAY NINE

BLESSED WITH HIS WORD

"Heaven and earth will disappear,
but my words will never disappear."
MATTHEW 24:35 NLT

I didn't grow up going to church or having anything to do with the day-to-day realities of faith or organized religion, other than making fun of it all every chance I got. As a result, when I was saved through a sovereign visitation of the Lord outside my cabin up in the woods of northwest Montana at the age of almost forty, pretty much all of Christianity was new to me, including the Bible.

I had seen a Bible before. I even tried to read a version of it when I was at university. I hadn't gotten much past the first few begats in Matthew 1 before it lost my interest.

Amazingly, after the Lord revealed himself to me in those woods, I became hungry for his Word. I would read my Bible every morning with a cup of tea or coffee and most every night before going to bed. It was exciting and amazing. So many of the passages I read thrilled me. However, at times, they also seemed almost too good to be true.

Was all of heaven really available to me here on the earth through Christ (Ephesians 1:3)?

Would the Lord truly never leave me nor forsake me (Deuteronomy 31:8)?

Had he really healed all my diseases (Psalm 103:3; 1 Peter 2:24)?

And given me authority over all the power of the enemy (Luke 10:19)?

One evening as I was pondering all of this, he whispered a question to my heart, *Do you know why the book in your hand is called my Word?*

I thought about it for a moment. I was aware that Christians referred to the Holy Bible as "the Word," but I had never thought about why.

That's when he told me, *Because I have given it to you. I have given you my Word. And I always keep my Word.*

Isn't that amazing? God has given us his Word. Literally. The Bible is a book of promises. All of them are true. You can count on all of them.

When others give you their word, it means that you are supposed to be able to count on them and that you can trust they will come through on their promises. That they'll stand by what they said.

Unfortunately, that had not always been my experience with people.

But when God spoke to my heart as a brand new believer that he had given me his Word, I knew I could trust him. I knew I could count on his promises. I knew he would keep his Word.

I even found later in Numbers 23:19 where he confirms this truth by promising that he is not a man that he should lie. That no matter what my experience had been with people not keeping their promises, I could be certain of every one of his—especially the ones that seemed too good to be true!

The Holy Bible is the Word of God. He has given you his Word. That means that you can be sure that every promise, every blessing, every gift, every miracle, every bit of it is for you. You can count on it. You can count on him. Because he is not a man that he should lie.

DECREES

I DECREE THAT:

1. God has given me his Word.
2. Every promise, every blessing, every gift, every miracle, every provision, every revelation, every bit of it is all for me.
3. God is not a man that he should lie.
4. I refuse doubt, uncertainty, and fear.
5. I trust God.
6. I believe his Word.
7. I claim it all as mine.
8. His Word is active and alive. It is all for me. It is at work in me. And it is being brought about for me.
9. Every day, as I am in God's Word, it gets into me, increasing my faith in the reality of all the he has done for me and all that he has given me. His promises will manifest in my life.
10. I stand on God's promises, certain that they will come to pass because he has given me his Word.

Decrees based on the following Scriptures: Matthew 24:35; 2 Samuel 7:28; Numbers 23:19; Psalm 9:10; Hebrews 4:12; Ezekiel 24:14; Romans 10:17

ACTIVATION

Every time you read your Bible and see a promise of God, claim it as your own. Attach your faith to it. See it as settled and established in your life. If you come across a promise that seems challenging to believe because of circumstances you are facing, remind yourself that God has not only given you the Holy Bible to share his truth with you but that he has also given you his Word to assure you that everything you see in the Bible is certainly yours.

_____

_____

_____

_____

_____

_____

_____

_____

_____

_____

DAY TEN

BLESSED WITH TRUTH

"But when He, the Spirit of truth, comes,
He will guide you into all the truth."

JOHN 16:13

The enemy is terrified of strong, righteous men. That's why he works over time to spread lies throughout culture about how men are the problem and that masculinity is toxic and that it would be better for the male half of the species to stop being, well, men.

Satan will also use challenges and disappointments from our personal history and experience to lie to us that the difficulties or hurts that we've known will always be our portion and that there's nothing we can do to change that.

The enemy wants us to feel powerless, broken, useless, and defeated because he is aware of the truth. He knows you are part of God's solution for this hour and that, as a Christian man, you are hell's worst nightmare.

The lies of the enemy will not stand because Jesus has given us his Holy Spirit, and one of the things that the Holy Spirit is brilliant at is leading us into all truth (John 16:13). Truth that shatters every lie of the enemy.

In 2019, I did a national Heroes Arise men's conference in the country of Cambodia. My heart went out to these men. They had been through so much in the past forty-five years. During the brutal, terror-filled reign of the Khmer Rouge, soldiers drove families from their homes, broke them apart, and placed them into forced labor camps. Anyone who resisted faced either execution on the spot or brutal slaughter in the killing fields. It was an unimaginably horrible time for everyone, but my heart especially broke for the men—the husbands and fathers. Imagine how emasculating it must have been to face the reality that either you allow the regime to break apart your family and enslave your wife and children or to gun down you and your loved ones in the streets. Think about how shattering it would be to realize there was nothing you could do to protect your home, your children, your wife, and even yourself. In many ways, the men of Cambodia are still living with the effects of that tragic history.

During our Heroes Arise event, we declared. In every message and ministry time, we reminded the men that their history was not their future and that in Christ they were not victims but victors. We helped them step into the truth that, as sons of God, they had the power to be difference-makers and solution-bringers in their lives, their families, and even their nation (2 Corinthians 5:17; Philippians 4:13). The message transformed these men!

Jesus Christ is the truth, the way, and the life (John 14:6). His truth of who you really are—despite any difficult history or disappointing circumstances—is your way into living the empowered life God created you for. His truth about your real identity as a son of God will shatter the lies of what others have said about you, what your circumstances have shouted at you, and even anything that you have chosen to mistakenly believe about yourself.

God begins the New Testament with an illustration of this truth. Matthew 1 starts out with the lineage of Jesus. It is an eye-opening history. There are well-known names like Abraham and King David, who were big deals but also had dark secrets (adultery, murder, and betrayal just to name a few). There are also names in the lineage of Jesus that no one has ever really heard of. People like Jeconiah and Eliud—ones that history would say are unknown or unimportant. Additionally, there are some truly scandalous names like Rahab the prostitute. Still, what we see from this history—

from any history—is that Jesus is well able to come forth and do something amazing!

Whatever your history, whatever your circumstances, whatever anyone has said about you, whatever lies you have been told or believed about yourself, the truth is that you are a son of God, you are mighty in him and made to do great works that bring him glory.

You are loved. You are accepted. You have a key role to play for the kingdom on the earth. There are great things coming for you.

That's the truth!

DECREES

I DECREE THAT:

1. The Holy Spirit is leading me into all truth.
2. Anywhere there is a lie in my life, the Holy Spirit is revealing it so that he can replace it by truth.
3. I will know the truth, and the truth will set me free from every lie of the enemy.
4. My past is not my future.
5. My history is not my destiny.
6. I am a new creation in Christ. The old things have passed away. I am coming into every good thing the Lord has for me.
7. I hold to God's truth. I walk in God's truth. I set my mind on God's truth.
8. I refuse every lie of the enemy, and by the grace of God, I bring every thought captive and into alignment with the truth of Christ Jesus.
9. The truth of God's Word renews my mind daily.
10. God has blessed me with his truth, and I choose to believe it.

Decrees based on the following Scriptures: John 16:13; John 8:32; 2 Corinthians 5:17; Philippians 4:8; 2 Corinthians 10:5; Romans 12:2

ACTIVATION

The Holy Spirit is here to lead you into all truth. He loves to do it, and he is really good at it. Ask him to show you an area where you have believed a lie about yourself. Maybe it's something negative that one of your parents or an authority figure said about you when you were young. Or perhaps it's some on-going circumstance that the enemy has used to get you to believe that things will always be that way. When the Holy Spirit highlights something to you, ask him to show you what the truth really is. And then invite him to lead you into that truth so it becomes firmly established in your life.

_____

_____

_____

_____

_____

_____

_____

_____

_____

BLESSED WITH JOY

There is a river whose streams make glad.

PSALM 46:4

When I lived in Montana, I loved to fly-fish. I got out on the river as often as I could. It was just a short drive in my old Cherokee from the cabin where I lived up in the woods. A lot of guys I knew liked to float the river when they fished it, but I liked to wade it. I liked to step right out into that river and feel its push while I worked my cast, mended my line, and waited for a big old rainbow trout to rise up and sip my favorite Parachute Adams pattern. Oh, it would make me smile. It would make me glad that the river was so close to me and that I could get to it so easily and so quickly.

That river was a blessing. It was a source of joy.

There's an even more amazing river available to you. One you can also step right into and wade out as deep as you want to go. You can get there even faster than I could get to those home waters of mine when I lived in Montana. As a matter of fact, this amazing river comes to you. It has the ability to put a bigger smile on your face, and in your heart, than anything of this world ever could.

It's the river of Psalm 46:4. It flows right out of heaven, and it brings gladness to the dwelling place of God, which, of course, is you.

That river of heaven that is constantly available to you—that streams into the very depths of you—is the Holy Spirit. The reason it "makes glad" is because, according to Galatians 5:22, one of the aspects of the Holy Spirit that he is flooding you with is joy!

This is why the apostle Paul told us to rejoice in the Lord in all things at all times and to dip back into that joy again and again (Philippians 4:4). This wasn't a command or even a suggestion. It was an invitation. Paul was letting us know that in the Lord there is a constant source of joy way bigger, way more certain, and way more powerful than anything the world can offer. We can partake of it any time we want, over and over again. Not only because joy feels good and brings hope and healing and bounty (Proverbs 17:22; 15:13, 15) but also because it is a source of strength for us (Nehemiah 8:10). Joy empowers us!

Happiness is situational. It is a mood that comes and goes based on our circumstances.

Joy is transformational. It is a fruit of the Spirit and a blessing from God that is always available to us at any time and in any situation. All we have to do is receive as it flows into us. When we do, the joy of the Lord heartens, heals, cheers, encourages, strengthens, and empowers us. We go from being affected by our circumstances to being affective in our circumstances. We go from feeling like victims to knowing that we are victors in Christ. It's easy. And it makes those around us hungry to know a God who blesses with such joy even in the midst of challenges.

It has been way too long since I have been fly-fishing. In truth, though, all I need to do to get back out on those waters is take some time and head to the river. It's a simple choice.

It's the same with the joy of the Lord. All you need to do is choose to go to that river of Psalm 46:4 and wade in. Heck, you're already there. God has blessed you with joy. All you need to do is turn your attention to it and receive.

DECREES

I Decree That:

1. There is a river of joy that flows straight from heaven into the very core of my being. It makes me glad!

2. Nothing can stop or slow this river. It flows fully and freely into the very core of my being.

3. I partake of the joy of the Lord. I drink deeply of it.

4. The joy of the Lord brings healing to me.

5. The joy of the Lord restores my soul and is medicine to my body.

6. The joy of the Lord is my strength.

7. The joy of the Lord heartens and encourages me.

8. I rejoice in the Lord and all his goodness. And again, I rejoice.

9. I not only receive from this joy-filled river of gladness, I share it with everyone I meet. I pour out joy everywhere I go.

10. The Lord has blessed me with joy!

Decrees based on the following Scriptures: Psalm 46:4; Proverbs 15:13, 15; 17:22; Nehemiah 8:10; Philippians 4:4; John 7:38

ACTIVATION

Smile. This is one of the easiest, simplest, and most powerful ways to tap into the river of joy that is flowing from heaven into your innermost being. Science has shown that the connection between positive feelings and smiling may be a two-way street. In other words, when we feel positive, we tend to smile. Also, when we choose to smile, we can actually nudge ourselves to feel positive. Add to this the kingdom reality that there's a river of joy flowing into you from heaven, and smiling becomes an easy activation to tap into your divine source of inner joy. Simply take a few moments and focus on God. If the difficult circumstances that are trying to steal your joy come back to mind, push them away by thinking about God's goodness, his love, and all his other amazing qualities. As you do this, let a smile rise up from your heart and spread across your face.

_____

_____

_____

_____

_____

_____

_____

_____

Blessed with Victory

But thanks be to God,
who always leads us in triumph in Christ.

2 Corinthians 2:14

Imagine if you went to Vegas and never lost a hand at the blackjack table or if you won every spin of the roulette wheel and every pull on a slot machine. It wouldn't take long before the casino boss hauled you into a back room to figure out how you had rigged the system. You could tell them, "I'm not cheating. That's just the way it is. I never lose!" No way they'd believe you. They'd kick you out of the place and probably have you run out of town as well.

But in God's kingdom, that's exactly how it is. It's all rigged in your favor. You never lose because Jesus has already won it all for you. He has blessed you with victory.

In 1 John 3:8, we read that the Son of God came for the purpose of defeating every work of the enemy. So when Jesus said, "It is finished!" (John 19:30), he meant he had absolutely accomplished the job of completely, utterly, and totally defeating any and every plot, ploy, attack, and assignment of the enemy.

If that wasn't enough, 2 Corinthians 2:14 makes it clear that God will lead you into that total victory in all things at all times. Whatever you are facing. Regardless of how long you have been facing it. It is done and defeated. The Lord has won the battle for you. He will find a way to bring you into that triumph no matter what.

To put it another way, the enemy doesn't get to win. He can't win. He's already defeated. The challenge is that sometimes it doesn't look and feel that way. That's where those first two words of 2 Corinthians 2:14 come in: "but" and "thanks."

In any given moment, it may seem like you are not winning. It may seem like finances are short, that the latest medical report is negative, that your company passed you over for a promotion, or that your prodigal is getting further and further away from the Lord. *But* that's just in the moment. The truth is that God *is* leading you in triumph. Always. When you have circumstances that are screaming that you do not have victory, you can yell right back at them, "Oh, but I do!"

If you are wrestling with your "but"—if you still have trouble believing that truly God is leading you in triumph despite your current circumstances—then it is time to give thanks.

Why do we say "thank you" to someone? It's because they have done something for us or given something to us. Jesus has done it all for us and has given everything to us. When we give him thanks, we are agreeing with that truth. Giving him thanks agrees with the complete, utter, and total triumph of the cross. Giving him thanks for what you choose to believe he has done, even if you do not see it yet, keeps you free from a victim mentality and helps you always walk in the victory Christ has given you (1 Thessalonians 5:18).

The promise is not that you will always feel victorious. The promise is, no matter what battle you are facing, in Christ you already have the victory. Your "but" and your "thanks" are ways God will lead you in triumph as you come into the full manifestation of the reality that "it is finished!"

The next time you find yourself in a battle, remember two important things. First, Christ has already won the battle. Second, the Lord *is* leading you in triumph because he has blessed you with victory.

DECREES

I DECREE THAT:

1. The enemy is not winning. In Christ, I already have the victory.
2. The Lord is leading me in triumph.
3. I am a victor in Christ. Every one of my circumstances must align with the total victory of the finished work of the cross.
4. God is for me, and he is with me. None can stand against me.
5. I am more than a conqueror in Christ because Jesus has already conquered every work of the enemy.
6. Jesus has disarmed and defeated every power, principality, plot, and ploy of the enemy. He has rendered them all null and void by his total victory over them on the cross.
7. I will not be afraid. I will not feel discouraged. I will stand in the strength of the Lord and watch him bring me into triumph, for the battle is the Lord's and he has already won it!
8. The Lord fights for me. The enemy I face today is defeated and shall be utterly destroyed.
9. No enemy will be able to stand against me because the Lord is with me, and he never fails or forsakes me.
10. Jesus has done all and won all. I am blessed with victory!

Decrees based on the following Scriptures: 2 Corinthians 2:14; 1 John 3:8; Romans 8:31, 37; Colossians 2:15; 2 Chronicles 20:15; 1 Samuel 17:47; Exodus 14:13–14, 28; Joshua 1:3, 5

ACTIVATION

Never mistake a battle for a defeat. Battles are how we take territory and advance the kingdom on the earth. God's people have always had battles in this world, but Jesus has overcome the world (John 16:33). When we walk with him, we are blessed with victory in our battles. Whatever battle you are in right now, give God thanks for the opportunity to take territory with him and for him. Give him thanks that he has given you victory in those battles and that he is leading you in triumph. Whenever a temporary circumstance tries to convince you that you do not have victory in a certain area, use your "but" to remind yourself that oh yes, you do. For example, if it is a health battle you are facing, give God thanks that he is your healer (Exodus 15:26). Give him thanks that you *are* healed by his stripes (1 Peter 2:24). When a symptom manifests in your body, declare, *Yes, I am overcoming (symptom) at this time, but the Lord is leading me into the triumph of divine health!*

_____

_____

_____

_____

_____

_____

_____

BLESSED TO BE A FATHER

"He that has seen me has seen the Father."
JOHN 14:9 NKJV

When our heavenly Father made us in his image, one of the greatest gifts he also gave us is to be able to reproduce in our own likeness. As men, God blessed us to be fathers. We have the amazing privilege of bringing forth sons and daughters. We get to protect them, provide for them, pour into them, educate them, share wisdom and insights with them, and most of all, we get to love and accept them unconditionally so that through us they get their first experience of the certainty of God's love.

The Lord has not only blessed us to be fathers. He has also blessed us to show our children the Father through how we love them.

One of the best fathers I know is my friend Darren Stott. He is the lead pastor of the thriving Seattle Revival Center. He is involved in his city's government. He is an author and itinerant speaker. He appears on and produces Christian and secular media (check out his *Supernaturalist Podcast Show*). He is also a very committed husband and father who is as focused on growing in his ability to love his four kids as he is on growing in his ministry and calling.

Recently, Darren shared with me about how important it is for dads to be there for their kids even in the seemingly simplest ways. When Darren's son Peter was in first grade, he shared with his class that his favorite thing to do was to wrestle with his dad. When Darren found out, he was surprised and honored. He hadn't realized how much Peter enjoyed their simple times of tussling on the floor.

Then one day, during one of their playful wrestling sessions, Darren accidentally slipped out of Peter's grip when he was pulling on Darren's arm. This sent Peter tumbling backward, and he bumped into the coffee table. Instead of immediately comforting Peter, Darren tried to get him to shake off the bump and jump right back into the fray. As a dad, he wanted to help his son learn to press on and fight back when things get a bit hard. Instead, Peter got angry and yelled at Darren, "No! I am done wrestling with you! I don't want to wrestle you ever again!"

At this point, Darren realized that it wasn't just that Peter had gotten a bump, but also something in his heart had been hurt. Darren dropped every agenda other than making his son feel loved, accepted, safe, and comforted. He gave him a big hug, told him that he was sorry that he had been hurt, and re-established the connection between him and his son.

There would be plenty of time and opportunities for Darren to teach Peter important lessons on persevering and overcoming. In that moment, Darren realized that what really mattered was that Peter knew he was loved. As a dad, Darren knew the most important thing he could do for his child was to show him the unconditional love of the Father.

God loves us when we win our battles. God loves us when we struggle in our battles. God loves us on our good days and on our bad days.

Fathers are blessed with the opportunity to love their children as the Father loves us. None of us will do it perfectly. None of us will always get it right in every situation. Fortunately, if we embrace this blessing of fatherhood and grab hold of the opportunities to make it more about connection and relationship than teaching or lecturing, our kids will always be willing to listen when we have wisdom to share.

As Darren put it when he told me this story, "Being a father has taught me that being right isn't my primary objective as a parent. My role is to pursue the hearts of my children in the same way that Father God pursues me."

DECREES

I DECREE THAT:

1. I am a son of God. My heavenly Father is always faithful to be present for me no matter what I am facing.
2. God the Father is with me in pain and difficulties. In those moments, he pours out his love upon me and shows me his Fatherly faithfulness.
3. Relationships matter to Father God. He made me in his image. He is teaching me to be the same kind of father to my children as he is to me.
4. I will protect my connection and intimacy with the Lord and with my family.
5. My children are a blessing from the Lord.
6. I will be present for my children.
7. I will be interested and involved in the lives of my children.
8. The only perfect father is Father God. I remove the yoke of impossible expectations to be an infallible father. I receive the grace of Father God to be a good father and to parent my children to the very best of my abilities.
9. I am committed to revealing the love, wisdom, joy, provision, and protection of Father God to my children by being the best reflection of him that I can be.
10. I am blessed to be a father.

Decrees based on the following Scriptures: Romans 8:29; Deuteronomy 31:8; Genesis 1:26; Psalm 127:3–4; John 14:9

Activation

Ask the Holy Spirit to reveal to you what activities really matter to your children. Schedule a meaningful one-on-one connection activity with each of your children. Sincerely express your heart to connect. Ask questions. Enjoy the moment. If necessary, repent for any times you have failed to be present. Make sure to let your children know how blessed you feel to be their dad.

_____

_____

_____

_____

_____

_____

_____

_____

_____

_____

_____

BLESSED WITH MIRACLES

"Truly, truly, I say to you, he who believes in Me,
the works that I do, he will do also;
and greater works than these he will do."

JOHN 14:12

You are not normal. You really aren't. You are way beyond normal. You are supernatural. You are a worker of miracles.

Here's how scripture puts it: you are in this world but not of it (John 17:16). As soon as you said yes to Jesus Christ, you were plugged into the kingdom of heaven. In Christ and through the indwelling power of his Holy Spirit, you now have the ability to put the reality of that kingdom on display here on the earth.

I want you to notice that I said you *are* supernatural. I didn't say you will *feel* supernatural. You might, on occasion, get the charismatic goosebumps and feel the Holy Spirit stirring up in you. You might, every so often, feel holy fire in your belly and healing power in your hands. If you do, great. Go with it. The important thing for you to understand is that you don't need to feel supernatural to be supernatural. You *are* supernatural. You simply need to step out into it.

I think we'd all agree that God is supernatural. Old Testament. New Testament. It is one supernatural act after another. If you took all the miracles, healings, deliverances, divine utterances, multiplications, angelic visitations, signs, and wonders out of the Bible, it would be more of a pamphlet than a book.

That supernatural God made you in his image (Genesis 1:26–28).

If that wasn't enough to convince you, Jesus himself comes right out and says that if you believe in him, you will do the works that he did (John 14:12). In Matthew 10:7–8, he gets even more specific when he commissions you to declare that wherever you go, the kingdom of heaven is at hand—your hand—and that you can heal the sick, cleanse the lepers, cast out demons, and raise the dead. In other words, you are supernatural and are blessed to work miracles.

You can't do it in your own power, but the good news is you don't have to. He has given you his Holy Spirit who comes to fill you all in all to do exceedingly, abundantly beyond your ability to ask, think, or even comprehend (John 15:26; 1 Corinthians 6:19; Ephesians 3:20). He empowers you to move in the miraculous (Galatians 3:5; Acts 1:8; Zechariah 4:6).

It says so right in 1 Corinthians 12:10. The Holy Spirit has given you the gift of "the working of miracles." The key is in that word "working." In the Greek, it is from the root word *energeo* that means both "to be mighty" and "to be active." If you want to be mighty in the working of miracles, you need to be active in the working of miracles. It is that simple.

God did it through Philip in the city of Samaria. The people paid attention to all that Philip shared because of the mighty miracles that he worked (Acts 8:6).

God did extraordinary and unusual miracles through the hands of Paul, and it caused many to turn to the Lord (19:11, 20).

Now he wants to do it through you. Get out there and be the supernatural expression of the kingdom of God on the earth you are meant to be. God has blessed you with miracles!

DECREES

I DECREE THAT:

1. I am a miracle-working explosion of God's kingdom on the earth.
2. I will do the works that Jesus did because I believe in him and believe that his Holy Spirit dwells within me.
3. God extends his hand through me to save, heal, and deliver.
4. Wherever I am, the kingdom of heaven is at hand.
5. I will heal the sick, cleanse the lepers, cast out demons, and raise the dead.
6. I am anointed with the Holy Spirit and with power. I go about doing good, healing, and delivering all who are oppressed of the enemy because God is with me.
7. The Spirit of the Lord is upon me. I will allow him to highlight the sick, hurting, trapped, broken bodies and souls that he wants to heal and deliver through me.
8. The Holy Spirit gives me miracle-working power to bear mighty witness of Jesus Christ everywhere I go.
9. The Lord works notable and remarkable miracles through me.
10. The supernatural is an everyday part of my life because I am blessed with miracles.

Decrees based on the following Scriptures: John 14:12; Acts 4:30; Matthew 10:7–8; Acts 10:38; Isaiah 61:1; Ephesians 3:19–20; Acts 1:8; 19:11; 1 Corinthians 12:10

ACTIVATION

Be active in the working of miracles so that you grow mighty in the working of miracles. The next time you see others who are sick or downcast or who have a walker, crutches, or cast, ask them what is going on with them. Listen to their stories. Let them share what they are dealing with. Then ask if you can pray for them. You know that Jesus paid the price for them to be set free from every sickness and affliction. He wants them to know it. He wants to work through you to reveal that truth through a miracle. If God instantly heals the next person you pray for, praise God. If you do not immediately see a result, don't feel discouraged. Find someone else to pray for. As you are active in the working of miracles, you will grow mighty in the working of miracles!

_____

_____

_____

_____

_____

_____

_____

_____

BLESSED WITH CHARACTER AND INTEGRITY

You are living letters written by Christ,
not with ink but by the Spirit of the Living God.

2 CORINTHIANS 3:3 TPT

Jesus declared, "He who has seen Me has seen the Father" (John 14:9). The apostle Paul echoed this truth in his letter to the Colossians when he shared that a significant part of Jesus's ministry was to be the visible representation of the invisible God (Colossians 1:15). In other words, one of the main reasons Jesus manifested on the earth was to put his Father on display for all to see.

As sons of God, you and I are called to a similar ministry. Jesus himself told us this in John 14:12 when he reminded every believer that we are to do the works that he did.

What that means is that, in Christ, you and I have the power to reveal the Father to everyone we meet just like Jesus did. Yes, this definitely includes working miracles, healing the sick, raising the dead, casting out demons, and proclaiming the truth of the gospel in power (Matthew 10:8). We will encounter people who have no interest in hearing us preach and no desire for us to pray for them. These are the ones whom the church has hurt, wounded, or disappointed. They may not be open to hearing about our God, but we can still reveal him to them by the way we live and how we treat people. This is the blessing of having his character and nature imbue us through the indwelling of his Holy Spirit. This is the witness of being men of godly character and integrity.

Here's how a friend of mine puts it, "We may be the only Bible some people ever read." In the words of the apostle Paul, you are an "epistle" read of all men (2 Corinthians 3:2 NKJV). This is not about a microscope of scrutiny or pressure to behave in certain ways. It's about the opportunity we have through the indwelling of the Holy Spirit to look and sound different than the selfish ways of the world. When we grab hold of that opportunity and choose to live with the character and integrity of Christ, we put the transforming reality of our God on display for all to see.

People at your work. Unbelievers in your family. Doubters out in the world. They may seem to have no interest in your faith or what you have to say about God. They may roll their eyes when they see your Bible or hear you listening to worship music. Still, they will take note of how you behave. Over time, they'll notice that you are different. They will notice that you are honest, kind, patient, generous, hopeful, and positive. It will register that you keep your word, that you're trustworthy, humble, generous, and that you treat others with respect. They'll notice that you follow through on commitments, that you're are a man of no compromise, and that you choose to adhere and live by the tenets of your faith no matter what. They will also notice that when you do blow it, because we all do, you own up to it and apologize. It will all have an effect. It all puts God on display in a way that, for some, is as powerful as a miracle or an answered prayer.

God has blessed you with character and integrity. You reveal him to everyone around you every time you choose to operate in them.

DECREES

I DECREE THAT:

1. My heavenly Father made me in his image.
2. My Father and I are one. His nature is my nature. His character is my character.
3. I am patient, kind, loving, peaceful, faithful, and trustworthy.
4. I am humble and honest.
5. I keep my word and operate in self-control.
6. I am courteous, thoughtful, and generous.
7. I am a man of complete integrity. I stay away from evil.
8. I am a divine portrait of my heavenly Father. The choices I make, the words I speak, the way I carry myself, and how I treat others all put him on display wherever I go.
9. My Father has imbued me with his very nature.
10. He has blessed me with character and integrity.

Decrees based on the following Scriptures: Genesis 1:26; John 10:30; Galatians 5:22; 1 Corinthians 13:4–7; Job 1:1; Colossians 1:15

ACTIVATION

Think of someone you know who has no interest in hearing about Jesus. Is it someone in your family? Someone at work? A friend you knew from before you were a Christian? Realize that how you treat them and behave around them can be as powerful a witness as sharing the truth of the gospel with them. Think of something kind or generous you can do that would put the character and nature of the Father on display for them the next time you see them. Do this before each interaction you have with this person. It will have an impact.

_____

_____

_____

_____

_____

_____

_____

_____

_____

_____

Day Sixteen

Blessed to Champion Women

I commend to you our sister Phoebe, a deacon of the church in Cenchreae. I ask you to receive her in the Lord in a way worthy of his people and to give her any help she may need.

ROMANS 16:1–2 NIV

Dr. Brian Simmons is one of my modern-day heroes of the faith. For decades, he worked as a linguist with New Tribes Missions to bring the gospel to unreached people groups around the world. He is the author of the brilliant Passion Translation of the Bible. He is an amazing preacher and teacher. Perhaps one of the most inspiring things about him is that he is committed to empowering not only men but also women in their gifts and callings.

As men, we are blessed by God to be champions of women, just as Jesus was.

Years ago, I heard Dr. Simmons share a powerful message out of John 4 about Jesus and the woman at the well. History tells us that her name was Photini. When she encountered Jesus, Photini was a woman whom society had marginalized and dismissed because of her scandalous past. No one saw any real value in her. No one, that is, but Jesus. He took the time to talk with her. He took the time to address the issues of her life and the issues of her heart. He spoke truth to her in love. She came to know him as Messiah. She became a powerful evangelist and revivalist who led her entire village to the Lord (v. 29). The writings of the early fathers of the faith tell us that Photini went on to spark revival in many more villages throughout the Middle East. Her name was mentioned among great early church pillars like Peter, James, and John.

Dr. Simmons pointed out in his message that we, as the body of Christ, are incomplete without our sisters inhabiting their roles as apostles, prophets, evangelists, teachers, and pastors. John 4:5–30 and Genesis 1 indicate that God feels the same way.

When God created us in his image and put us in place as his dominion stewards on the earth, he created us male *and* female. He is very specific about that in Genesis 1:27. Men are part of the plan and so are women. The fullest, truest, and most complete representation of God on the earth is when both men *and* women are operating in their divine authority in every sphere of influence.

For far too long and in far too many segments of the church, we have limited women in where we have allowed them to serve. There is nothing wrong with a woman serving as a pastor's wife or a Sunday school teacher. If it is her calling, then it is truly glorious. However, God calls many of our sisters to something different. As men of God, we are blessed to come alongside of them in those callings. We have the blessing to help them identify and develop their spiritual gifts and to support and cheer them on as they step out to move in them—with no agenda other than seeing them walk in the fullness of all they were created for in and out of the church.

In John 20:11–18, we see the risen Lord help Mary step out into an apostolic preaching ministry (vv. 17–18).

Peter, James, John, and the other early disciples served alongside of many called and anointed sisters.

The apostle Paul cheered on women like Priscilla, Junia, Euodia, Mary, Tryphena, Tryphosa, Phoebe, and Chloe. We see in Romans 16:1–2 that Paul not only named Chloe a deacon in the church, but he also asked others to come alongside of all she was called to do for Christ. He championed her!

Speaking of the apostle Paul, there has been quite a bit of controversy and misunderstanding about his counsel to Timothy in regards to women. In 1 Timothy 2:9–15, Paul was helping his young leader figure out how to best deal with the issues of women in the church of a city renowned for its Diana cults and priestesses. If this counsel was meant as some kind of global restriction of women, it would have been in direct conflict with Paul's other writings and instructions honoring women as teachers and leaders. (If you have questions about this, I highly recommend the insights Loren Cunningham shares in his book *Why Not Women?*)

Throughout the Bible, we see the Lord use women to achieve his divine purposes on the earth. In the Gospels, we see Jesus include and empower women. As men of God, we are blessed to see the very best in our wives, daughters, sisters, and the women we serve and worship alongside of. We are blessed to cheer on and champion the women in our lives!

DECREES

I DECREE THAT:

1. When God made us in his image, he made us male and female.

2. The fullest and most complete representation of God on the earth is when both men and women are moving in the fullness of their gifts and callings.

3. As a man of God, I am called to be a champion of virtuous women.

4. I see and celebrate the gifts and talents of the women in my life, in my church, and in the body of Christ.

5. The church needs women. Women are necessary. Women have an important role to play for the kingdom on the earth.

6. I am proud to serve with, serve alongside of, and serve under the women around me whom the Lord has called and anointed.

7. When it comes to gifts, talents, and callings, there is no male or female in Christ Jesus; there are simply those who are willing to serve and bring glory to the Lord.

8. I celebrate the gift to the world and to the church that women are.

9. God created my sisters in the body of Christ to do his good works and bring him glory.

10. I cheer on women. I cheer for women. I am blessed to be a champion of women.

Decrees based on the following Scriptures: Genesis 1:27; Galatians 3:28; Ephesians 2:10

ACTIVATION

Think of a virtuous woman that you know. Ask the Lord to give you a word of encouragement for her. Email or text the word to her, letting her know that as her brother in Christ, you believe in her and are cheering her on.

_____

_____

_____

_____

_____

_____

_____

_____

_____

_____

_____

_____

Blessed with Abundance

*"I have come to give you everything in abundance,
more than you expect—life in its fullness until you overflow!"*
John 10:10 TPT

Somewhere along the way, a lie crept into the church that poverty is holy. I think it's because we have confused the truth that the *love of money* is the root of all evil (1 Timothy 6:10) with a misconception that money itself is evil. Money is simply a resource. It is not good or bad in itself. It is really about our view of money and our relationship with it. God does not want us to see money as our security or source. He wants us to know that he is our security and source. He wants us to realize that he has blessed us with an overflowing abundance of every good thing.

If poverty were holy, if it were a good thing, why would God want us to look after the poor (Proverbs 22:9; 31:20; Deuteronomy 15:7; Galatians 2:10; 1 Timothy 5:3)? If lack were something we were to aspire to, why would the Lord ask us to help those who are in lack? Why would he say in Deuteronomy 15:4 that there should be no poor among us?

I have served in many cities, regions, and nations wracked with poverty. I have been among people ravaged by extreme lack. There is nothing holy or good about it. There is nothing of it that looks or feels like heaven on earth. It is devastating—both physically and emotionally.

Our God is not a God of lack. He is a God of abundance. All the silver and all the gold are his (Haggai 2:8). The entire world and all it contains are his (Psalm 50:10–11). Every good and perfect thing belongs to him, and he freely gives them (James 1:17). Since day six, his plan has been for us to be in relationship with him, and in that relationship, he would bless us with abundance (Genesis 1:29; 2:9). From that abundance, we are to steward all creation. We are to be a blessing because we are blessed (1:28).

Jesus came to restore us to that place of plenty. He says so right in John 10:10. He came so that we might have abundance. Second Peter 1:3 echoes this where we see that in Christ, we have been blessed with *everything* pertaining to life and godliness. Now that's abundance!

Blessing us with everything is one of God's "precious and magnificent promises." This abundance in him actually helps us "escape the corruption that is in the world" (2 Peter 1:4). Isn't that amazing? The abundance that the Lord blesses us with keeps us free from the wickedness of the world. The plenty of God that is ours in Christ keeps us free from evil. This is because when we know we have all we need in him—an abundance of every good thing—there is no need for us to seek what the world has to offer. It has nothing we need because he has blessed us with an abundant overflow!

Lack in any area—finances, favor, joy, peace, vigor, friends, love— is not your portion. Lack is not what God has blessed you with. If you are lacking in any area, it is because the enemy has been stealing from you (John 10:10). Today that stops. Today you see that God has blessed you with abundance—an overflow of every good thing, everywhere you need it. Today the thief has been caught, and you can claim a sevenfold payback (Proverbs 6:31). Today you recover all (1 Samuel 30:8).

In Matthew 6, when Jesus is reassuring us that our heavenly Father has more than taken care of all our needs here on the earth, he tells us the key to tapping into this abundance. It is to seek first his kingdom. When we do, everything we could ever need will be ours. As Jesus puts it, "all" will be added (v. 33).

The Lord isn't telling us to get our eyes off the things that we need in this world and to forget about them and accept lack. He is not saying that if we are good Christians and deny ourselves things like delicious food and nice clothing that we will earn something from God. He is reminding us that when we turn our attention to God and his abundant kingdom that Christ has restored us to, we will realize we already have an overflow of every good thing. He wants us to see it so that we can claim that abundance in every area of our lives, expecting it to be added because God has blessed us with abundance!

DECREES

I DECREE THAT:

1. Jesus came so that I will have an abundance of every good thing in my life.
2. I am overflowing with abundance in every area.
3. God has blessed me with an abundance of finances.
4. God has blessed me with an abundance of peace, joy, favor, love, patience, goodness, gentleness, faithfulness, self-control, and kindness.
5. God has blessed me with an abundance of health, life, strength, vigor, and vitality.
6. God has blessed me with an abundance of wisdom, insight, and understanding.
7. In Christ, I have everything that pertains to life and godliness. Whatever I need in this life, God has given it to me in Christ.
8. No area of my life is in lack. I will prosper and know plenty for all of my days. My finances, family and relationships, work, health, faith, and devotional times and intimacy with the Lord are all abundantly blessed.
9. I set my eyes, my heart, and my thoughts on the kingdom of God. I am a son of God. Everything in his realm is already mine. All that I will ever need has been added to me in Christ.
10. I am overflowing with blessings because the Lord has blessed me with abundance.

Decrees based on the following Scriptures: John 10:10; Galatians 5:22; Romans 8:11; Proverbs 3:13; 2 Peter 1:3; Deuteronomy 15:4; Matthew 6:33; Luke 15:31

ACTIVATION

Is there an area where it looks and feels like you have been in lack? Perhaps it is finances, or maybe it is one of the other areas we looked at—peace, joy, wisdom, patience. Take time today to repent for having accepted this as your portion up until now. If you have ever murmured or complained about suffering lack in that area, repent for being negative as opposed to standing in your place of authority in Christ to call in your portion of plenty. Then speak to that area. Declare that the thief has been caught, that he may no longer steal from you, and call in your sevenfold return. Every day speak to that area of your life, call it blessed, and declare that it is abundant and overflowing.

_____

_____

_____

_____

_____

_____

_____

_____

Day Eighteen

Blessed with Courage

"Have I not commanded you? Be strong and of good courage."
Joshua 1:9 NKJV

In May 2014, I was in Bangkok praying and preparing to lead a week of meetings and outreaches. During the time while I was there, a coup broke out. As soon as I saw on the news what was happening, I went right to the center of where the violence was so that I could find a high place in the midst of it all and make scriptural decrees into the spiritual atmosphere of the city and the nation. I remember hearing the crack of gunfire and finding out later that less than one hundred feet from where I was, people had been shot and killed. I was aware of the situation and even aware that there was danger. But more than any of that, I was aware that God had placed me in that city at that time and for a purpose.

I have been in other situations where I was very aware that there was danger all around me. Still, I was able to do what God had sent me there to do. I believe it was because God blessed me with courage.

I'm sure you have heard the expression, "Whom God appoints, God anoints." In other words, if God calls you to do something, he will give you what you need to do it. Part of that will be courage to say yes, to step out, to keep at it, to believe in his truth and his promises, and, yes, to move past any fear or intimidation in order to do what needs doing.

The promise of God blessing us with courage is right there in Joshua 1:9 where he reminds us that he has "commanded" us to be courageous. Now in English, we could read that word "commanded" as God demanding that we be courageous or that he is placing an expectation upon us to whip up some courage via our own moxie. However, in the original Hebrew, the meaning is clearer. The word is *tsavah*, and it can be translated as "to appoint" and "to send with." So what God is really reminding Joshua here is that when he appoints us to do something, he sends us forth with the courage to see it through. We don't need to stir up courage on our own; God actually blesses us with the courage we need for anything he invites us to do.

I remember the first time I was invited to sit in as a guest host for a popular show on GodTV. The regular host called me up and asked if I could come into the studio that morning to do some filming. My first thought was, *Are you nuts?* I had done some media over the years and had even been a guest on this very show several times, but to come in with no preparation and off-the-cuff lead a show that would go out to tens of millions of people around the world? I let them know that I really appreciated the opportunity, but I didn't feel like I had the prep time I would need to do a good job for them.

As soon as I hung up, the Holy Spirit spoke to my heart to not give in to fear. He let me know that while I might not feel ready, he was and he would be with me. I called the host back and said I would do it and that I would get to the studio as soon as possible. The Lord blessed me with the courage to say yes, the courage to trust that he would lead me and put his words in my mouth, and the courage to push away any fear and doubt as I drove over to the studio and got ready to do the show. It went great, and I went on to guest host for them many more times.

If God appoints us to do something, he will bless us with the courage to see it through.

For you, it might not be going into the middle of a military overthrow to speak out the truth of a nation's destiny or to step out into a media calling. Still, it will be something that feels beyond you, and the Lord will bless you with the courage you need to step into it and see it through.

It might be staying in a difficult marriage long enough for God to heal it and transform it.

It could be continuing to believe for your prodigal even though he seems to be getting further and further from the Lord.

Perhaps it will be starting up a new business that the Lord has given you an idea for even in the midst of a challenging economy.

Whatever it is, the Lord is with you, and he will bless you with courage.

DECREES

I DECREE THAT:

1. The Lord is with me. He will not fail me. He gives me all I need for every situation I face.

2. I will not be afraid. I will not feel discouraged. My confidence is in the Lord, and he gives me courage.

3. I will stand firm in the Lord. I will let nothing move me from his plans and purposes. I give myself fully to all he has called me to do.

4. I give no place to fear. The Lord is leading me. He is with me. I will not be put to shame.

5. My heart is not troubled. I am not afraid. I can do all things through Christ who strengthens me.

6. I put my trust in the Lord. I trust his word. I trust his truth. I trust that he is with me and that he is making me brave.

7. I am on guard against fear and doubt. I give no place to them. I am courageous.

8. I fear not because I only believe.

9. I have not received a spirit of fear but one of love, power, and self-control. I cast down all intimidation.

10. I will keep moving forward. I will keep learning. I will keep growing. I will keep saying yes to all God has for me. Because the Lord has blessed me with courage.

Decrees based on the following Scriptures: Joshua 1:9; 1 Corinthians 15:58; Isaiah 54:4; John 14:27; Philippians 4:13; Psalm 56:3–4; 1 Corinthians 16:13; Mark 5:36; 2 Timothy 1:7

ACTIVATION

Where do you need courage right now? Bring that situation before the Lord and thank him for giving you all the courage you need to step out and see it through. Take some time to bind fear and cast down intimidation. Even more, by faith receive the courage with which the Lord is blessing you, strengthening you, and sending you forth.

DAY NINETEEN

BLESSED WITH WEAPONS OF WARFARE

For the weapons of our warfare are not carnal
but mighty in God for pulling down strongholds.

2 CORINTHIANS 10:4

Back in the early 1990s, a friend of mine was a young Air Force pilot flying missions in Operation Desert Storm. Because of his involvement, I paid a lot of attention to the news during the build up to the Gulf War. I remember that whenever the media mentioned the Iraqi Republican Guard, they always described it as an "elite, war-hardened" fighting force—an enemy to be feared. Reporters talked about their strength, preparedness, and effectiveness in an almost legendary tone.

When it came time for the actual battle, it was hardly any fight at all. United States ground forces rolled through the Republican Guard with almost no resistance. Many of those "elite" troops simply laid down their arms and surrendered.

The legend was an illusion. The truth was that our troops were much better prepared and much better equipped with much better weapons of warfare. The enemy saw this and simply gave up.

It's similar for you and me in Christ. The enemy tries to convince us that he is mighty. The devil wants us to think that he is some great threat. The truth is that Jesus has already defeated him (1 John 3:8; John 19:10; Colossians 2:15). If that wasn't enough, in Christ, we not only have the victory, but we also have amazing weapons of warfare that empower us to walk in that victory!

In Ephesians 6:10–17, the apostle Paul tells us all about the weapons of warfare God has blessed us with, or, as Paul refers to them, "the full armor of God." These include:

- Belt of truth
- Breastplate of righteousness
- Sandals of peace
- Shield of faith
- Helmet of salvation
- Sword of the Spirit

These weapons are not carnal (2 Corinthians 10:4). In other words, they are not actual physical armaments, but they are real. They are mighty, and they outfit us to walk in the victory Christ has given us. When we take up these weapons of warfare, we are actually putting ourselves inside of Christ and his total triumph over every work of the enemy.

Jesus is the truth that girds up our loins and keeps us from stumbling over any lie the enemy tries to poison us with. Jesus is our imputed righteousness that keeps the wickedness of satan from entering our hearts and affecting our restored relationship with our heavenly Father. Jesus is the Prince of Peace who crushes the enemy beneath our feet as we walk with him (Romans 16:20). He is the author of our faith who protects us from the fiery darts of fear, doubt, and unbelief that the enemy launches against us. He is our salvation that renews our minds and fills our thoughts with godly revelation, insight, truth, and wisdom that keeps us free from the corruption of the fallen world. Jesus is the Word of God and the Sword of the Spirit that we wield against the enemy to cut down every one of satan's attacks.

The next time it feels like you are in a battle, remember that you are actually in Christ. Jesus Christ has already defeated the enemy. You have the victory. Jesus has blessed you with the most powerful weapons of warfare imaginable so that you can always walk in total triumph.

DECREES

I Decree That:

1. The Lord has blessed me with everything I need to walk in victory.

2. I put on the full armor of God.

3. I am girded up with the belt of truth. Every lie of the enemy is exposed and defeated. The truth of the Lord strengthens and encourages me.

4. I put on the breastplate of righteousness. I am holy as Christ is holy. I am pure as Christ is pure. I submit no part of me to wickedness.

5. My feet are shod with the readiness of the gospel of peace. I walk with the Prince of Peace. Fear and anxiety have no place in me.

6. I take up the shield of faith. I do not live according to my feelings or understanding. I live by faith.

7. I put on the helmet of salvation. I guard my mind against the lies of the enemy. Every thought I have is that of a beloved son in whom his Father is well pleased.

8. I wield the sword of the Spirit, the Word of God. I arm myself by reading and declaring the truth of God's Word.

9. I stand victorious in the Lord. Christ has defeated the enemy.

10. The Lord has blessed me with weapons of warfare. I am victorious in Christ.

Decrees based on the following Scriptures: Ephesians 6:10–17; John 14:30; 1 Peter 1:16; Romans 6:13; 16:20; Mark 5:36; 1:11; 2 Corinthians 10:5

ACTIVATION

Put on the full armor of God. Take the time to pray through Ephesians 6:10–17. As you do, see yourself actually putting on your divine armor and taking up your heavenly weapons. Know that as you go out into your day today, you are covered, protected, and empowered. You are mighty in the Lord and ready for whatever comes your way!

Blessed with Peace

The peace of God, which surpasses all understanding,
will guard your hearts and minds.

Philippians 4:7 NKJV

In John 20, the disciples were literally locked up in fear.
Scripture tells us that they were meeting behind locked doors
because they were afraid (John 20:19). They didn't understand
what was going on. They didn't understand why Jesus had been
arrested, beaten, tried, and executed. They didn't understand why
he hadn't done what they had expected him to do. They felt like
everything they had been working toward for the last three years
had come to nothing. To their minds, the future was uncertain.
They were totally freaked out.

Can you relate? Have you ever found yourself in circumstances
that felt way beyond your understanding? A situation you just can't
get your head around? One that even had you questioning if God
was there or if he cared?

He is. He does. And he has a gift for you in those situations:
Peace!

- A peace that passes all understanding (Philippians 4:7).

- A supernatural peace that is greater than your circumstances and even greater than your need to understand
  what is going on.

- A peace that will center you back in the truth that he loves you, is there for you, and has good things for you no matter how it all might look or feel in the moment.

- A peace that will help you step past fear, doubt, or anxiety and continue forward into the glorious future he has for you.

Let's go back to John 20. The disciples were freaking out because their circumstances seemed well out of their control. It all felt way beyond their capabilities. This is when Jesus—the risen victorious Lord—showed up. He stepped through the walls and declared, "Peace be with you" (v. 19).

Jesus didn't declare, "Here is some peace, I sure hope it helps." He supernaturally stepped into all that they were facing and worried about and declared the certainty that peace *was* with them. Jesus is the Prince of Peace (Isaiah 9:6). He was releasing the revelation that he who is Peace was right there for them. He was opening their eyes to the reality that they didn't need to understand their circumstances. What they needed was to understand that he who has won all, done all, and is above all was right there in the midst of what they were facing.

The disciples got it. They chose to believe that despite all that had happened and all that was going on, Jesus, the Prince of Peace, was there with them. Fear fell away, and they were filled with joy (John 20:20). Their circumstances hadn't changed. They still didn't really understand what was going on, but now they understood that no matter what, Jesus was with them. This is the peace that passes all understanding. It is the truth that God is there, that he cares, and that he is on the job. Even if we don't see it, feel it, or understand what the heck is going on.

True peace never comes from our circumstances. Even when everything looks and feels good in the moment. Peace is not a situation. Peace is a person. That means you can always have peace because you always have Jesus (Matthew 28:20).

No matter what you are dealing with, what you are feeling, or how difficult, complicated, or confusing it all may seem, you can be at peace because the victorious risen Lord is right there in the thick of it all with you. It might not always look like it or feel like it, and it might not always make any sense, but it doesn't need to. Because the peace that he has blessed you with, the peace that allows you to trust him and continue to move forward with him, surpasses all understanding.

DECREES

I DECREE THAT:

1. Jesus is the Prince of Peace. He stands with me in every situation I am facing.

2. Even when I do not understand my circumstances, I understand that the Lord is with me, he is for me, and he is leading me into the glorious future he has for me.

3. I am anxious for nothing. The peace of God, which surpasses all my understanding, guards my heart and mind.

4. The God of peace is crushing satan beneath my feet as I continue to rest in Jesus, trust in Jesus, and move forward with Jesus.

5. Jesus is stepping through any walls of fear that have kept me locked up in doubt or anxiety. He is releasing peace to me right now. I receive his peace.

6. The peace of Christ rules within me.

7. My mind is at peace in Christ. My heart is at peace in Christ. My soul and body are at peace in Christ. He keeps me in his perfect peace.

8. For all of my days and in whatever I face, I am at rest in the peace of the Lord.

9. I trust in the Lord, and he multiplies his peace for me.

10. My heart is not troubled. I am not afraid. The Lord has blessed me with peace.

Decrees based on the following Scriptures: Isaiah 9:6; Philippians 4:7; Romans 16:20; John 20:19; Colossians 3:15; Isaiah 26:3; Proverbs 3:2; John 14:27

ACTIVATION

Are you anxious about anything? Concerned? Afraid, even? Invite Jesus to step into the situation that seems the most beyond your understanding right now. Turn it all over to the Prince of Peace. Let him know you don't know what to do, and remind yourself that you don't need to; you simply need to know that he is with you. Take a deep breath. As you inhale, imagine yourself being filled with the peace he has for you. As you exhale, let go of all tension, fear, doubt, and worry.

_____

_____

_____

_____

_____

_____

_____

_____

_____

_____

Blessed with Glory

*"The glory which You have given Me I have given to them,
that they may be one, just as We are one."*

John 17:22

Just before Jesus went to the cross, he declared that he was blessing us with the very same glory that the Father had given him while he was on the earth. He also declared why he was blessing us with the glory of God, which was a very specific reason. It was so that we could each be one with the Father just as Jesus was one with him.

Think about that: *just as one.* Now that is amazing!

When Jesus was fulfilling his purpose as the Son of Man here on the earth on our behalf, he was still fully the Son of God in perfect union, communion, friendship, and fellowship with his heavenly Father. The key to this was the glory.

The glory has been described as many things. The presence of God. The atmosphere of heaven here on the earth. In reality, our ability to sense and experience those things are the result of us having the glory. They are the result of us being one with the Father even as Jesus was one with him.

What exactly is this "glory" he has blessed us with? How does it allow us to be so fully and completely one with the Father in all things at all times?

We see the answer in Exodus 33:19. When Moses asks God to show him his glory, the Lord replies by declaring that he "will make *all of My goodness* pass before you." The glory of God is the fullness of his goodness.

When Jesus says that he will give us the very same glory the Father gave to him, he is declaring that in him we receive the same revelation and awareness of the Father's goodness in all things at all times that he had while he was here on the earth.

The Son of Man went through a lot of tests, trials, temptations, and challenges on our behalf. He faced a barrage of difficulties, betrayals, slander, abuse, and unfair treatment. At times, he even cried out because it was all so intense (Matthew 26:38–39; Luke 22:42–44). Yet, never once did the Son of Man doubt the goodness of the Father. He remained the Son of God throughout it all, certain that his Father was with him, was for him, and was working on his behalf to bring about glorious victory even in the midst of severe challenges. The Son of Man walked as the Son of God here on the earth because of his revelation of the fullness of the Father's goodness in all that he faced. Never once did he doubt or pull back from the Father. Every moment he was here on the earth, Jesus was one with the Father because of the glory.

Now he gives that glory—that same revelation of the fullness of the Father's goodness—to you so that you can be just as one with him as Jesus was when he was on the earth.

When we go through tests, trials, and challenges, the enemy works overtime to get us to doubt that God is there and that he cares. Satan knows the Father will never withdraw from us, so he tempts us to withdraw from the Father. The enemy wants us to pull away in the hard times and give in to fear, anxiety, or our own tactics as opposed to trusting in the will and ways of the Father. When we have the revelation of the fullness of the Father's goodness, we will never pull away from him. Even in challenging times, we will press in. We will double down on trusting our gloriously good and gloriously trustworthy Father in heaven. We will remain one with him, knowing that he is good and knowing he will bring about a good result from our current set of circumstances.

You are a son of God. Because of the Son, you have been blessed with the glory. You are one with the Father just as Jesus was one with the Father. In all things, at all times, you can always expect the fullness of his goodness.

DECREES

I DECREE THAT:

1. Jesus has given me the very same glory that the heavenly Father gave to him. By faith, I receive the glory of God.

2. I am one with the Father just as Jesus was one with him.

3. I am a son of God, immersed in his glory. Every moment of every day, I am in union, communion, friendship, and fellowship with my heavenly Father.

4. I have the revelation of the fullness of his goodness in all things and at all times.

5. I trust that my heavenly Father is good.

6. I am certain that I will see the goodness of my God here on the earth.

7. God is making all of his goodness pass before me. I am constantly in the presence of the fullness of God's goodness.

8. God is good, and his loving kindness is everlasting. He never stops revealing his goodness to me.

9. Nothing will cause me to doubt or pull back from my God. I trust that he is there. I trust that he cares. I also trust that he is at work bringing about the very best results from my current set of circumstances.

10. The Lord has blessed me with his glory. I am one with him.

Decrees based on the following Scriptures: John 17:22; Psalm 27:13; Exodus 33:19

ACTIVATION

You are one with the Father just as Jesus was one with him. Jesus often took time out from the busyness of the day to connect one-on-one with the Father and enjoy the specialness of their relationship. Take the next fifteen minutes to simply sit and talk with the Father. Speak to him as if he is right there with you because he is. The more you acknowledge and invest time in your relationship of oneness with the Father, the more you will experience the reality of his presence and be aware of the fullness of his goodness.

_____

_____

_____

_____

_____

_____

_____

_____

_____

BLESSED WITH INCREASE

*"Do not despise these small beginnings,
for the Lord rejoices to see the work begin."*
ZECHARIAH 4:10 NLT

The kingdom is funny. Often the biggest things start out in the seemingly smallest of ways.

That's why the prophet Zechariah tells us not to despise small beginnings. Because in the kingdom, a small beginning does not mean you'll end up with a small portion. Just the opposite really. Embracing small beginnings and stewarding what you have with care and wisdom are keys to great increase in the kingdom.

Think about the coming of Messiah. The single biggest, greatest, most significant thing to ever happen in the history of the world began in such a small way that almost everyone missed it.

The Savior of all could have begun on the earth any way he wanted to. He could have come as a mighty warrior accompanied by legions of angels that trumpeted his certain triumph or as a conquering king, resplendent in regalia and announced with pomp and circumstance. He could have made a huge deal of it. Instead, the Son of God, who came as the Son of Man, started out on the earth as a tiny baby born in such humble conditions that only his parents, a few desert nomads, and some livestock took notice. It was such a small beginning that almost everyone he came for missed it. Of course, it didn't stay small. Increase came.

The kingdom work that almost no one noticed when it started increased to affect everyone, everywhere, for all of time.

You want to talk about a small beginning? When God called me into full-time ministry, I was forty years old and had only been saved for about nine months. I heeded the call with excitement and expectation, leaving behind literally every aspect of the past four decades of my life other than what fit in my old Jeep Cherokee that I used to drive down to Arizona to be part of starting up the US branch of a Canadian ministry. God had shown me my call to preach, to be a prophetic voice to the nations, and to carry revival everywhere I went. It started with me moving into an old, single-wide trailer in an asphalt parking lot in a sketchy area of Mesa, Arizona. It was literally a small beginning—about 240-square-feet small.

After quite some time of serving faithfully behind the scenes, I did my first meeting. I think there were just over a dozen people there. I preached my heart out. To me, it was not about the size of the crowd; it was about the size of the opportunity to share the word of the Lord and see people impacted by his presence, power, and truth. I trusted him to bring the increase. And he did. Over the years, opportunities came for me to speak at conferences and events. Doors began to open for me in the nations. I was asked to appear on Christian TV and streaming media, and words that I carried went out to millions of people around the world.

Proverbs 28:20 promises that "a faithful man will abound with blessing." If we are faithful to what God calls us to, increase will come.

When it comes to something that starts small, don't focus on the "small." Instead, focus on the "start." Begin. Step out. Be faithful. The Lord will bless you with increase.

DECREES

I DECREE THAT:

1. Thank you, Lord, that you rejoice in the work that I have begun with you and for you.

2. Thank you for being with me every step of the way.

3. I have been faithful to what the Lord has called me. Because I have been faithful, he is blessing me with more. More opportunity. More favor. More grace. More reach and influence. More resources.

4. Right now, the Lord is increasing me. He is stretching forth my tent pegs. He is expanding me to the right and to the left.

5. God is giving me a greater capacity to be blessed and to be a blessing. He is enlarging my territory. He is bringing increase.

6. All of my works are blessed. All of my holdings are multiplying.

7. I abound with blessing and am constantly being increased.

8. Every one of my good works is multiplying. Every one of my storehouses is overflowing.

9. The Lord is increasing me more and more. All of my household and I are being blessed, increased, and multiplied.

10. In every area where I have been faithful, the Lord rejoices, and he blesses me with increase.

Decrees based on the following Scriptures: Zechariah 4:10; Matthew 25:21; Isaiah 54:2; 1 Chronicles 4:10; 1 Corinthians 3:7; Proverbs 28:20; Psalm 115:14–15

ACTIVATION

When you start a new work with the Lord, turn it over to him. A simple but powerful way to do this is to take communion and dedicate the work unto the Lord. Whether it is a new business, a new job, or stepping into a new aspect of your calling, declare that you have begun the work for him and with him. Let him know that you trust him to bring the increase.

DAY TWENTY-THREE

BLESSED WITH SUCCESS

"You will prosper and succeed in all you do."

JOSHUA 1:8 NLT

God made you for success. God made you to come out on top in every situation (Deuteronomy 28:13). God made you to be fruitful and multiply (Genesis 1:28). God made you to rule and reign (v. 28). God made you to prosper (Jeremiah 29:11). There is no one who wants to see you succeed more than the Lord, which only makes sense considering he's your heavenly Father. He loves you. He has nothing but good things for you. He has blessed you with everything you need to succeed.

Do you need wisdom? Done (James 1:5).

Do you need strategies and guidelines? Done (Joshua 1:8).

Do you need resources? Done (Philippians 4:19).

Do you need favor? Done (Proverbs 3:4).

Do you need connections in high places? Done (Ephesians 2:6).

Do you need someone to go before you and open doors? Done (Isaiah 45:2).

God is more committed to your success than even you are. He promises in Deuteronomy 28 that if you heed his counsel, he will command his blessing upon whatever you put your hand to (vv. 1, 8).

He did it for David. It says so right there in 1 Samuel 18:14, "David succeeded in all his undertakings because the Lord was with him." Just like the Lord is with you. God doesn't show favoritism (Acts 10:34–35). What he does for one, he does for all.

He is simply looking for someone who is willing to walk with him, talk with him, and follow his lead. Like it says in Joshua 1:7–8, pay attention to his word, obey it, and you will have success wherever you go.

In the Lord, you have all you need to succeed. That means you never have to fear failure. Not because you won't ever fail but because you know that failure is not your portion. It's not your ultimate destination. Failure is simply a temporary setback. One that you'll learn from, grow from, and move on from.

If right now you're in the midst of a real challenge or even something that looks and feels like an epic failure, think about the disciples. After Jesus was arrested, tried, found guilty, and crucified, they thought everything had gone totally sideways. To them, Jesus hanging on the cross and going into the tomb was a total failure. They came to find out it was anything but. It was all actually a set-up for the greatest success of all time.

Sometimes in the kingdom, that's how things work. What feels like an obstacle ends up becoming a launching pad. What looks like a failure is simply a temporary delay along the way to your success.

The key? Keep moving forward with God. Keep walking with him. Keep heeding his counsel. No matter what. The only way things don't work out is if you give up and quit, so don't.

Put your hand to the plow. Keep your eyes on the Lord. Follow his lead and keep at it. He will bless what you put your hands to. So get back to it and expect for it to ultimately all work out. The Lord has blessed you with success.

DECREES

I DECREE THAT:

1. In Christ, I have everything I need to succeed.

2. The Lord is with me. He prospers me in all that he calls me to do.

3. I read and study the Word of God. I meditate on his counsel. Because of this, I am certain to succeed.

4. The Lord commands his blessing upon me.

5. Everything I set my hand to is blessed, successful, and bears good fruit.

6. I am successful in my work. I am successful in my relationships. I am successful in my investments. I am successful in my spiritual growth. Every area of my life is blessed and prosperous.

7. I am the head and not the tail. I am above and not beneath. I am more than a conqueror.

8. When I ask for wisdom, the Lord gives it to me. Wisdom gives me the advantage to be successful in every area of my life and in all that I do.

9. I am with God, and he is with me. He will never stop until he brings me into all he has promised me. I will not give up.

10. I am diligent. I learn from any mistakes or setbacks. I continue on with the Lord. Everything ultimately works out for me because the Lord has blessed me with success.

*Decrees based on the following Scriptures: 1 Samuel 18:14;
Joshua 1:7–8; Deuteronomy 28:8; Psalm 1:3; Deuteronomy 28:13;
Ecclesiastes 10:10; Genesis 28:15*

ACTIVATION

Have you hit what feels like a roadblock? Are you in the midst of what looks to be a setback? Remember, ultimately it will all work out. God made you for success. The Lord is with you. Ask him what he wants you to learn from where you are right now. Ask what he has for you that you weren't aware you needed until you were in this situation. This is all part of the journey. Heed his counsel, and he will bless what you put your hand to.

BLESSED TO BE A HUSBAND

He who finds a wife finds a good thing.
PROVERBS 18:22

Back before my wife and I had even met, a friend gave me some advice about being a husband. He said that when I met the right woman, if I went into marriage with any other expectation than that it was God's perfect creation to help me die to myself and learn to love unconditionally, I would be disappointed. He told me this was coming from a man who had been married to his best friend for more than thirty years and that she was the greatest gift God had ever blessed him with.

My first thought was, *Wow. That's not very romantic.* Over many years of being married, however, I have come to discover that he was right and that despite my initial reaction, this insight is actually the key to real romance. It is about *true* love that commits to loving through every set of circumstances and that prefers another over yourself. Love that values what you can selflessly give more than what you could selfishly demand. Love that never stops loving. Love that loves how Jesus, the ultimate bridegroom, loves. Learning to love like this really is the gift of marriage and the blessing of being a husband.

I think this is what Proverbs 18:22 is getting at when it tells us men that when we find a wife, we find a good "thing." A good wife is a wonderful blessing, for sure. I know. The Lord has blessed me with one. However, a wife is not a *thing*. I think the good *thing* we find in marriage is the opportunity to love someone unconditionally and unselfishly. As the apostle Paul puts it in Ephesians 5:25, *"Husbands, love your wives, just as Christ also loved the church and gave himself up for her."*

None of this is to say that as husbands we won't "get" anything out of marriage. It's to help open our eyes to the realization that getting the opportunity to learn to love like Jesus is the ultimate blessing of being a husband. I can tell you from my own experience, the more we husbands learn to give our wives the certainty of love, the more love, romance, respect, appreciation, intimacy, and sex we are likely to receive. Funny how that works. The more we demand those things, the more they seem to diminish over the years. On the other hand, when we go out of our way to love our wives no matter what, all of a sudden, there's no need to demand anything because they feel safe to freely give everything.

My wife is amazing. I wouldn't be the man that I am if I hadn't met her and married her. Part of that is because she is so smart, funny, wise, beautiful, fun, and generous. It's also because, as good as our life together is, it's not perfect. There have been challenges. There have been disagreements. But those haven't been negatives. They have been opportunities to grow, to choose love, to become more like Jesus, and in that, to see our marriage, our friendship, and our connection grow even deeper and truer. That's the blessing of being a husband.

DECREES

I DECREE THAT:

1. The banner over my marriage is love.
2. My wife is a blessing and a gift, and I will think of her, speak to her, and speak about her with love, honor, and respect.
3. By the grace of God, I will love my wife as Christ loves me and as he loves his church.
4. I embrace the good thing that my marriage is. I celebrate my marriage. Even on the days when there are challenges, I rejoice in the blessing of being a husband.
5. Jesus is my model of what it is to be a bridegroom. Every day I will grow in love.
6. Every day Christ conforms me more and more into his image, and my marriage is going from glory to glory.
7. I am committed to my wife in good times and bad.
8. God turns all things to the good. When my wife and I have a disagreement, it is not a bad thing. It is an opportunity to grow in love and grown closer with one another.
9. I count it a joy to be the spiritual head of my household and establish an atmosphere of love, honor, and respect in our home and in our marriage.
10. The Lord has blessed me to be a husband.

Decrees based on the following Scriptures: Song of Solomon 2:4; Proverbs 31:10; Ephesians 5:25; Proverbs 18:22; Romans 8:29; 2 Corinthians 3:18; Romans 8:28; Ephesians 5:22–23; Hebrews 12:2

ACTIVATION

Jesus is our ultimate example of a bridegroom. The next time you and your wife have a disagreement, instead of giving into the temptation of getting mad or frustrated, choose to see it as an opportunity to grow in love—a chance to be more conformed into the image of Christ. Ask the Lord how he would approach it. What would it look like to love as he loves in this set of circumstances? How would he share his heart? What words would he use? You have every right to be heard and for your views and feelings to be considered. So does your wife. By approaching the discussion as Jesus would, you will help create an atmosphere where you both find it easier and more constructive to work through challenges and come out stronger on the other side.

BLESSED WITH RIGHTEOUSNESS

His faithfulness, not ours, has saved us,
and we have received God's perfect righteousness.

GALATIANS 2:16 TPT

Jesus came to restore you to all that Adam and Eve lost in the garden. When you said yes to him and received Jesus Christ as your Lord and Savior, he restored you to the fullness of relationship with your heavenly Father. He brought you back into the place of being made in his image and representing him on the earth, including his character and nature. Thanks to Jesus, you have been made the very righteousness of God in Christ (2 Corinthians 5:21).

What is most amazing to me about this is that we *are* his very righteousness. It is not something we need to do. It is not something we need to make happen now that we're saved. Jesus has done it for us. He *has made us righteous*. We simply need to agree with this truth and allow it to come forth.

My good friend Brad Carter oversees Calvary Wallace, a thriving multi-cultural church in North Carolina. He works with a network of fellowships and is an integral part of all that we are doing through Men on the Frontlines. He is a great guy to speak to our men around the world because he himself is a man of integrity who has learned to so powerfully embrace the blessing of righteousness in Christ.

Before Brad became a believer and apostolic minister, he was a football coach. As many of you know, that world is often full of rough language. Brad was no exception. When he received Christ, he suddenly had a desire to change how he spoke as a reflection of what God had done in his life.

For several weeks, Brad tried really hard not to curse (Ephesians 4:29). What he found was that the more he focused on what he was not supposed to do, the more he seemed to do it. Not swearing became almost impossible for him.

The Father started to speak to his heart. He kept reminding Brad who he really was in Christ. He spoke wisdom to him, saying, *Instead of focusing on what you think you shouldn't say or do so you can be a better Christian, why don't you focus on what my Son has done for you because you are already righteous in him!*

That was the revelation Brad needed. He realized that he didn't have to make himself righteous; he already was the very righteousness of God in Christ. Jesus had done it for him. So he began to focus on who he truly was as opposed to what he felt he should or shouldn't say and do. More and more, his behavior and language began to change. He began representing ("re-presenting") his Father and the new creation he truly was in Christ because he realized this is who he really was.

When Brad and I were talking about this, he shared with me, "Whenever I find myself at a place of temptation, instead of thinking and declaring, *I need to be righteous, so don't do that unrighteous thing*, I think and declare, *I am the very righteousness of God in Christ. I don't give into temptation because I am righteous.* Not by my works but by the work of Jesus!"

Amen, brother.

You don't need to make yourself righteous. You couldn't if you tried. Jesus has done it for you. He has blessed you with righteousness. You simply need to agree with this new reality and allow it to come forth in your life.

DECREES

I DECREE THAT:

1. I am the very righteousness of God in Christ.
2. The Lord has wrapped me in a robe of his righteousness.
3. Old things have passed away. I am a new creation.
4. My thoughts are righteous.
5. My words are righteous.
6. My actions are righteous.
7. My decisions are righteous.
8. I am holy as he is holy. I am righteous as he is righteous.
9. Every day, I become a greater and greater representation of my heavenly Father. This is not by my doing but by the power of his Holy Spirit within me.
10. The Lord has blessed me with righteousness.

Decrees based on the following Scriptures: Galatians 2:16; 2 Corinthians 5:21; Isaiah 61:10; 1 Corinthians 1:30; 1 Peter 1:14–16; Zechariah 4:6

ACTIVATION

In any area where you wrestle with unrighteousness and have been trying to change your behavior, ask the Holy Spirit to reveal to you what God is like in those areas. Ask him to help you see in Scripture what Jesus was like. Next, focus on the fact that this is your new character and nature in Christ. Focus on that truth. Declare that truth. Let it become real to you. If you find yourself wrestling in that area again, don't give place to guilt and condemnation. Simply declare who you really are so that the wrong behavior begins to look and feel wrong to you. It will fall away because in Christ you are holy as he is holy and righteous as he is righteous.

BLESSED WITH SOLUTIONS

"He can interpret dreams, explain riddles,
and solve difficult problems."

DANIEL 5:12 NLT

Our God is very good at coming up with solutions. To show you just how amazing he is at dealing with even the most difficult of problems, consider this: the Lamb was slain before the foundation of the world was laid (Revelations 13:8). In other words, before Adam and Eve entered the world and before it even entered their minds to rebel against the Lord, God already had a solution in place to deal with the whole problem of the fall.

Nothing takes God by surprise. He is never left standing around thinking, *Wow! I did not see that coming!*

Not only does God have brilliant solutions for any and every situation, he freely shares them with us. All we ever have to do is ask him (James 1:5; Jeremiah 33:3). When you don't know what to do, rest easy because you know him. He has all the wisdom and insight you'll ever need to solve any problem you ever face.

I can be a bit of an absent-minded-professor type. I am often thinking of several things at once, and I am not always fully paying attention to what all is going on around me. Because of this, I have been known to set down my glasses and forget where I put them. For those of you who do not wear any kind of corrective lenses, let me explain the inherent challenge of having to look for a misplaced pair of glasses. You need your glasses to see where you left your glasses—talk about a catch-22!

This had been a recurring challenge for most of my life but not anymore. One morning about a year after coming to know the Lord, I was trying to find my glasses when all of a sudden the Holy Spirit spoke to my heart that he knew where they were. I thought, *Well, yeah, of course you do. You know everything.* Because he does (Hebrews 4:13; Psalm 147:5). I asked him where they were, and he showed me that they had fallen behind my bedside table. I went into the bedroom, reached back behind the table, and sure enough, there they were. Problem solved!

No challenge is too small or too big. He has the solution for whatever you face, from a misplaced pair of glasses to the scheming onslaught of a major demonic power.

Our ministry staff includes some of the most loving, kind, and amazing people I have ever known. Every one of them is committed to Jesus, committed to walking in kingdom values, and committed to serving together. On the rare occasion that an issue comes up within our team, everyone is very willing to honestly and humbly work through any misunderstandings so that we could all learn and grow together. Truly, they are a Matthew 18:15 company.

Then all of a sudden, we hit a season where one issue after another was coming up. Misunderstandings. Miscommunications. Hurt feelings. Offenses. Even more odd was that whenever we sat down to process through issues, we never could seem to get things resolved. It was actually just the opposite. The more we tried to help people work through the misunderstandings, the worse things got. It was not at all like our team. Another leader and I sought the Lord, and he revealed that what we were dealing with was an onslaught by the spirit of leviathan. He also gave twelve keys to overcoming this high-powered demonic spirit and to see it defeated in our midst. Over the next few months as we applied his solutions, everything shifted. Relationships were healed. Friendships were restored. Our ministry was stronger than ever.

I also came to discover that this assault of leviathan was not isolated to just us. It was actually a global attack against believers, churches, and ministries. I took the keys the Lord had given us and turned them into a book, a video series, and a manual that have now gone throughout the world. Almost everywhere I travel, people tell me that those keys gave them the enlightenment and empowerment they needed to realize what they had been dealing with and to overcome it. When we asked, God gave us the solution we needed and then helped turn that into a global solution for people everywhere who were dealing with leviathan.

Our God is brilliant, and no one is better at solving problems. All you ever have to do is ask, and he will bless you with solutions for whatever you are dealing with.

DECREES

I DECREE THAT:

1. My wise, wonderful God is never caught off guard or taken by surprise.
2. God always knows what to do.
3. He knows exactly what I am dealing with and exactly what I need.
4. When I ask him for wisdom, strategies, and solutions, he gives them to me.
5. The Lord is always willing to reveal his secrets to me and share kingdom strategies.
6. I posture myself to hear and receive the divine solutions I need to solve the situations I am facing. By faith, I receive them into my spirit right now.
7. God knows exactly what I need in all that I am dealing with.
8. I have the mind of Christ.
9. God has filled my understanding with divine knowledge and intelligence.
10. I am able to remain hopeful and solve even the most difficult problems because God is with me, and he has blessed me with solutions.

Decrees based on the following Scriptures: Hebrews 4:13; Psalm 147:5; Matthew 6:8; James 1:5; Jeremiah 33:3; Deuteronomy 29:29; 1 Corinthians 2:16; Daniel 1:17; 5:12

ACTIVATION

God promises that whenever you need wisdom, all you have to do is ask. Sit quietly, take communion, and bring before the Lord the challenge that you need a divine solution for. Thank the Lord for hearing your prayer and for giving you the wisdom you need to deal with what you are facing. Receive the solution by faith. Do not doubt.

_____

_____

_____

_____

_____

_____

_____

_____

_____

_____

_____

BLESSED WITH RESTORATION

"I will rebuild its ruins, and I will restore it."

ACTS 15:16

As men, we often want to ignore or just move on from wherever we feel have fallen short and things haven't worked out. However, God wants us to do the opposite. He wants us to bring to him anywhere there are "ruins" in our life—whether they're our fault, the fault of others, or simply the result of difficult circumstances. He wants to rebuild, restore, and redeem those places.

Our God is all about restoration. Jesus came to restore us to relationship with our heavenly Father. He restored us to our citizenship in the kingdom of heaven. He restored us to our authority as dominion stewards here on the earth. He restored us to eternal life in Christ. All that humanity lost at the fall Jesus has restored to us.

If he restored all of that for you when you were still lost in your sins, is it any wonder to find out that he blesses you with restoration in every area of your life now that you are his beloved son?

Is your marriage in ruins?

Are your finances a total mess?

Is your career completely stalled?

Is your business bankrupt?

Is your relationship with your kids non-existent?

God wants to restore them all! There is no area beyond

his reach. There is no wreck beyond his repair. There is no ruin beyond his ability to rebuild and restore.

For most of my life, my father and I really didn't connect. We were very different, and we never seemed to know how to be around one another. My sudden and radical conversion to charismatic Christianity through a sovereign visitation of the Lord at the age of almost forty didn't help things a whole lot. When my brilliant, MIT-engineer father found out, he thought his "weird" son had gone even further off the deep end, especially when I decided to give up everything—including a lucrative career on the creative side of big-budget advertising—to follow the leading of the Lord into a life of itinerant ministry. My father pretty much thought I had gone nuts and joined a cult.

You could easily say that my relationship with my dad was in ruins at that point. We barely spoke to one another, and the one time we did try to connect, I can sum up the visit by simply saying it did not go well.

I told myself that I was okay with it all. That I had tried, and it was what it was. The Lord, however, felt differently.

One morning, about a month before I was scheduled to be ordained, I was in prayer. The Lord spoke to me very clearly and told me to invite my father to the ordination ceremony. My first response was *No way!* My father had clearly communicated that he was uncomfortable with my faith, so I simply could not get my head around the idea of him attending a full-blown charismatic commissioning service complete with the laying on of hands and prophetic ministry.

I shared with the Lord that the ordination ceremony was something very special to me, something I had worked hard for, and that it meant a lot to me. I told him that it was my day, and I wanted to be able to fully enjoy it. He spoke again, gently but very clearly, reminding me that actually it was his day because he was commissioning me into a life of serving him in the five-fold ministry with all of my days for the rest of my life. He let me know that he wanted to invite my father to the ceremony, and then he shared the text for an email he invited me to send to my father.

I sent the email but was convinced that there was absolutely no way my father would even respond to it, let alone actually come to the ceremony. I was wrong on both counts.

I don't have room in this devotional to go into all the astounding things that happened over the next several weeks. Suffice it to say, the Lord used my ordination service to work a miracle of restoration between my dad and me. It was a total shift. I am grateful to tell you that since then, and to this day, we have only grown closer. We love, respect, and enjoy one another. My dad is one of my favorite people. There is no hint, and barely a remembrance, of all the years of disconnect between us.

Wherever there is "ruin" of any kind, anywhere in your life, bring it to the Lord. He will bless you with restoration.

DECREES

I DECREE THAT:

1. My God is a God of restoration. He is well able and absolutely willing to rebuild, redeem, and restore every area of my life where there is something broken, stalled, ruined, or wrecked.

2. God is restoring my finances.

3. God is restoring my health.

4. God is restoring my relationships.

5. God is restoring my spiritual inheritance and every blessing of my bloodline.

6. God is restoring my joy, peace, favor, authority, and influence.

7. God is restoring the fullness of my destiny and all that he knew and planned for me. Every blessing. Every bit of prosperity. Every hope. Every aspect of my future. God is restoring them all.

8. Wherever there was shame or disgrace in my background or my bloodline, God is moving. He is restoring. He is bringing me into a double portion and everlasting joy.

9. The resurrection power of God is reviving, healing, and restoring all areas of my life. He is making me strong, firm, and steadfast.

10. God has blessed me with restoration wherever there are ruins in my life.

Decrees based on the following Scriptures: Acts 15:16; Deuteronomy 30:3; Jeremiah 30:17; Psalm 51:12, 71:20–21; Jeremiah 29:11; Isaiah 61:7; Job 42:10; 1 Peter 5:10

ACTIVATION

Where are the ruins in your life? What is the hardest place for you to look at? What is the area that feels like your biggest failure? That's where God wants to reach in and bring restoration. No matter the reason. Whether it's your fault or someone else's. Whether it's the result of a mistake or even an injustice. God is bigger and well able to restore the situation and redeem the years. Bring those ruins to him. Invite him to move mightily in that area. Walk with him step by step in whatever he shows you to do— even if your role is simply to release it to him completely and do nothing except trust that he will restore all.

_____

_____

_____

_____

_____

_____

_____

_____

_____

_____

Day Twenty-Eight

Blessed with Perfect Prayers

The one who speaks in tongues
advances his own spiritual progress.

1 Corinthians 14:4 TPT

In Matthew 21:22, Jesus is mentoring the disciples on the power of prayer. He tells them, "If you believe, you will receive whatever you ask for in prayer." How amazing is that? Jesus is letting us all know that faith-filled prayer is the key to receiving *everything* the Father has for us here on the earth.

You've already experienced this. Think of your salvation. At that moment when you realized that Jesus did truly give his life for you, you believed. You prayed the prayer of salvation in faith, and you received eternal life in Christ. It is the same for every good thing the Father has for you and everything he wants to release through you. Whether it's provision, protection, promotion, power, breakthrough, healing, miracles, resurrection, transformation, favor, or wisdom, you name it. The way you receive it is to know it is for you and ask for it in prayer.

What about the things of 1 Corinthians 2:9? According to that scripture verse, God has prepared things for you that "eye has not seen" and "ear has not heard," amazing things you haven't even imagined yet. How can you ask for something you have not seen or heard? How can you put into words, let alone a prayer, a faith-filled request for something you've never thought of or even imagined?

Don't worry. God, in his goodness, has provided for you here as well. He has blessed you with the ability to pray perfect prayers through the gift of tongues.

Tongues is a heavenly language that you receive directly into your born-again spirit through the indwelling of the Holy Spirit of God (12:10). This divinely supernatural language allows you to pray in the spirit above and beyond anything you could ever think to pray in your earthly language. With tongues you can pray for things your natural eye, ear, and mind have not ever seen, heard, or thought of because these prayers are not inspired by your understanding; the Holy Spirit of God inspires them.

When you pray in tongues, you are praying prayers that are in perfect agreement with the plans and purposes of God, even those plans and purposes you have no natural understanding or concept of yet.

About six months into being a new believer, I had a sovereign encounter with the Lord where he took me into a vision and baptized me in the Holy Spirit. During this encounter, he also gave me the first few words of my heavenly language. Soon after that, I came across a book called *The Hidden Power of Speaking in Tongues* by Mahesh Chavda. In it, Mahesh shared all about the power of the gift of tongues. He also mentioned that committing to praying in the spirit for thirty minutes a day for forty days in a row would birth amazing things of God in a believer's life. I was hungry for everything the Lord had for me, so I took up the challenge and prayed in tongues for at least a half hour a day for the next forty days.

During that month and a half, while I was praying in tongues, I rarely sensed much of anything going on. That is the funny thing about tongues. Its power is not in our understanding or in what we might see or feel when we are praying in the spirit. The power of tongues is to pray deep unto deep, Spirit to spirit, divinely inspired prayers in perfect agreement with the will and ways of God.

It was not long after those forty days of focused praying in tongues that my life radically changed. I received my call into full time ministry. God connected me with my mentors, Ron and Patricia King. After a few months of doing prophetic and miracle evangelism with them out on the streets, they invited me to move down to Phoenix and help them launch the US arm of our ministry. I traveled with them full time and then launched out into a global itinerant ministry under their covering. I had not heard, seen, or even imagined any of that, but I know it all came forth from those forty days of perfect prayers!

The apostle Paul told the church, "I wish you all spoke in tongues" (14:5). Paul knew that when we pray in tongues, we speak forth the mysteries of the kingdom here on the earth (v. 2). God has blessed you with this powerful gift of perfect prayers. Begin to put them to work in your life today, and start birthing the greater things he has for you!

DECREES

I DECREE THAT:

1. I believe in the Lord, and because of this, I speak in new tongues.
2. The Holy Spirit is stirring up this gift inside of me.
3. The Holy Spirit comes upon me and empowers me to pray in tongues.
4. When I pray in tongues, I am praying divinely inspired, perfect prayers.
5. When I pray in tongues, I am building myself up in my most holy faith.
6. When I pray in tongues, I am being edified and established in the greater things that God has for me.
7. I am calling forth what my eyes have not seen, my ears have not heard, and what has not even entered into my imagination every time I pray in tongues.
8. Thank you, God, that by your grace I will pray in tongues more and more.
9. When I do not know what to pray or how to pray, the Holy Spirit reminds me to pray in tongues.
10. God has blessed me with perfect prayers through the gift of praying in the spirit.

Decrees based on the following Scriptures: 1 Corinthians 12:10; Mark 16:7; Acts 19:6; 1 Corinthians 14:4; Jude 20; 1 Corinthians 2:9; 14:18; Romans 8:26

ACTIVATION

For the next week, commit to praying in tongues for a set amount of time each day. Try starting off with just five minutes. Then each week, add an additional five minutes. Do this until you are up to thirty minutes a day.

DAY TWENTY-NINE

BLESSED WITH HEALTH AND HEALING

"I am the Lord who heals you."

EXODUS 15:26 NKJV

When the Lord delivered his people out of the bondage of Egypt, it is estimated that their population was two million or more. It says in Scripture that not one of them was sick or feeble (Psalm 105:37). Think about that. Two million plus people is the size of a major metropolitan area. Astonishingly, every single one of them was healthy and strong.

This is what the Lord has for you as well. He has set you free from bondage. His blood has brought you out of the captivity of sin (Romans 6:6). Just like those Israelites, there is to be no sickness in your midst either. He shows us this truth all through the Bible.

Isaiah 53:5 promises us that Jesus not only paid for all our sins and iniquities but that he also has healed us of all our diseases.

In Psalm 91, the Lord promises us that he will allow no plague or pestilence to touch us or come near our house. If it tries to, we can call out to the Lord, and he will make us well (Psalm 30:2; 41:3).

Throughout the Gospels, Jesus puts the reality of his healing power on display again and again. Everywhere he went, everyone who came to him was made well (Matthew 4:14; 8:16). Often Jesus healed them in an instant, like with Peter's mother-in-law (8:14) or the man at the pool of Bethesda (John 5:8–9). Sometimes the healing manifested over time, like with the leper in Luke 17:12–16.

There were also times when the person laid hold of it by faith (Mark 5:25–34). Jesus healed them all.

I don't pretend to fully understand how God does things. Sometimes God heals instantly. Sometimes he heals over time. Sometimes he heals on this side of eternity. And sometimes he heals when he brings us home to glory. I'll leave the why of all that to him. All I know is that Jesus heals.

For many years, I was beset with a mysterious and debilitating illness. It was like having the worst flu you could imagine for more than a decade. Any type of activity would leave me in bed, weakened, exhausted, shaky, and burning with fever. No matter what or how much I ate, I kept withering away until I was a frail shadow of my former self. Every day, I would take authority over the un-named illness that was coming against me. Again and again, I would decree that Jesus Christ was above every sickness and disease and that I was healed by his stripes. Over and over, I declared that he is the Lord who heals. I did this week after week, month after month, and year after year. Often, my faith was strong. I knew God had healed me and that the symptoms must bow. Other times, I wrestled with discouragement, fear, and doubt.

One morning, on a day many years into the battle, I cried out to the Lord in frustration. I shared with him that it seemed like my prayers were not working and that no matter how many times I declared his eternal truth, nothing seemed to change. I dropped my head back on the cushion of my prayer chair, closed my eyes, and told the Lord I was weary. At that moment, I went into a vision. I saw myself many years in the future at the end of my time on the earth. The Lord was welcoming me into heaven and commending me on having run my race well. As we walked about, person after person came up to me, thanking me for when I ministered the healing power of Jesus to them. I did not recognize any of them. I turned to the Lord and asked him, "Who are all these people? I don't remember praying for any of them." The Lord looked deep into my eyes and told me that every time I proclaimed the truth that he is the Lord who heals, his power went forth and someone somewhere was set free from sickness. At that moment, I realized that every prayer has impact. His word never fails; it never returns void (Isaiah 55:11). Truly, he *is* the Lord who heals. It was not long after that vision that things began to turn around for me. Today, I am back to traveling the world, preaching, and ministering in strength.

Sickness is of the devil. It is not your portion. It is not allowed to stay.

Healing is of God. He has set you free from every sickness and disease. If healing comes instantly, praise God. If it comes over a matter of time, always remember that no matter how long you have had those symptoms, they are not yours. Keep going to Jesus with them. He has and he will take them from you. Keep giving them to him. Over and over if necessary. Keep expecting them to leave. They are a lie. Because the truth is this: God has blessed you with health and healing.

DECREES

I DECREE THAT:

1. The stripes of Jesus have healed me.
2. There is no sickness in my midst.
3. The very same spirit that raised Jesus from the dead dwells within me.
4. The Holy Spirit is lifting me up out of every sickness and symptom the enemy has sent against me.
5. The Holy Spirit is quickening my mortal body into divine health right now.
6. Every system, organ, gland, bone, nerve, tissue, joint, muscle, and fiber of my being God is healing and strengthening.
7. The blood of Jesus covers my body and soul; he has healed and delivered me.
8. I allow no sickness to be near me. I rebuke every disease, plague, infirmity, virus, negative bacteria, and disease sent against me. They must all bow to the name of Jesus and leave my midst now.
9. Jesus has given me an abundance of life, health, strength, vigor, and vitality. In his name, I command every sickness, symptom, pain, and problem to leave me now.
10. God has blessed me with health and healing.

Decrees based on the following Scriptures: Isaiah 53:5; Psalm 105:37; Romans 8:11; Exodus 15:26; Psalm 91:10; John 10:10

ACTIVATION

The Word promises that we will prosper and be in health as our souls prosper. Take some time today to sit with the Lord and invite him to minister to your soul. Let his love, peace, joy, and goodness melt away any stress, anxiety, or pressure that you have been holding onto. Take a deep breath. Let your muscles relax. Now invite the Holy Spirit to quicken your mortal body with the abundance of life Jesus came to give you (John 10:10). By faith, receive that health, strength, and vitality into any area of your body that needs healing.

_____

_____

_____

_____

_____

_____

_____

_____

_____

_____

Day Thirty

BLESSED WITH
BOLDNESS

But the righteous are as bold as a lion.

PROVERBS 28:1

I love teaching our schools on prophetic and power evangelism. It is so cool to see believers realize the power they have in Christ to put the kingdom of God on display. The students go from being hesitant and unsure to chomping at the bit to get out there. Sometimes it is hard to keep up with them on the streets because they are so excited to reach the next person and the next person and the next person. They can't wait to see God move.

That's where true boldness comes from.

Boldness is not being aggressive or brash. A bullhorn doesn't make you bold. It just makes you loud.

True boldness is a radical willingness to step out because you are expectantly confident that the Lord wants to show up.

When I need my boldness re-kindled, I often think of the encounter between Jesus and the leper in Matthew 8:1–3. All sorts of people surrounded Jesus. He was in the midst of a massive crowd, but the leper was the only one to approach him. I believe their conversation reveals the reason why. My favorite version of it is in the 1996 edition of New Living Translation. In that version, the leper says to Jesus, "Lord, if You want to, You can make me well again." Jesus touches him and says, *"I want to.* Be healed." Instantly, the leper was healed.

Of all the people crowded on that mountain to listen to Jesus as he taught, only one was bold enough to approach him, and only one sensed that the Lord *wanted* to heal him.

Knowing God can do something makes us expectant. Knowing God wants to makes us bold.

Ephesians 3:12 tells us that we have boldness in Christ. It goes on to reveal that because of this boldness, we can freely access our heavenly Father and all of his kingdom, and we can be assured of his glad welcome. We know he wants relationship with us. After all, that's why he sent the gift of his Son. That certainty allows us to be bold.

This is why in situations where the world shrinks back, the righteous are as bold as a lion (Proverbs 28:1). We know we are accepted in Christ. We know God loves us. We know we belong to our heavenly Father. Even more, we know our heavenly Father's heart. We know he can heal and save and deliver. More importantly, we know he wants to. We are certain of it.

That's why no matter where we are—whether it is out on the streets, at the grocery store, filling up at the gas station, or taking a coffee break at work—we can boldly be on the lookout for an opportunity for God to show up through us.

We can be boldly confident that he wants to reach the lost.

We can boldly expect that he wants to heal the sick.

We can boldly know that he wants to encourage the downcast.

Anywhere we see darkness that needs light, death that needs life, or a problem that needs a kingdom solution, we can confidently and expectantly step out because we know he can. We know he wants to. In that, the Lord has blessed us with boldness.

DECREES

I Decree That:

1. I am as bold as a lion.
2. I am confident that my God can and even more confident that he wants to.
3. My God wants to reach the lost. He wants to heal the sick. He wants to bring freedom to the oppressed. He wants to encourage the downcast. And he wants to do it through me.
4. Because of Christ and my faith in him, I boldly step out expecting him to show up in every situation.
5. I am the solution to any problem I encounter because Christ is in me and greater is he!
6. Thank you that you make me bold, oh Lord. Make me bold in sharing your truth. Make me bold in sharing your heart. Make me bold in sharing your presence. Make me bold in sharing your power.
7. Every day I grow bolder and bolder.
8. The Lord has not given me a spirit of fear but one of love and power that propels me to boldly share the kingdom with everyone I meet.
9. My confidence is not in myself; my confidence is in God. So I confidently step out wherever I am to put him and his kingdom boldly on display.
10. The Lord has blessed me with boldness.

Decrees based on the following Scriptures: Proverbs 28:1; Matthew 8:2–3; Ephesians 3:12; Philippians 4:13; 1 John 4:4; Acts 4:29–30; 2 Timothy 1:7

ACTIVATION

The next time you feel a nudge to step out—whether it is to share the Gospel with someone, pray for the sick, speak a word of encouragement, prophesy, or share Jesus in some other way—take just a moment before you do and reflect on the certainty that God wants to reach the person he is nudging you toward. Remember that he can save, heal, deliver, and encourage. Even more, he wants to. Let that certainty make you expectantly confident in God's heart for that person. Then boldly go to them.

DAY THIRTY-ONE

BLESSED WITH HEROIC HOLINESS

The entire universe is standing on tiptoe,
yearning to see the unveiling of God's glorious sons.
ROMANS 8:19 TPT

According to our Bible verse for today, all of creation is anxiously anticipating the sons of God realizing who they really are and stepping out into the authority we have in Christ to have a positive impact on the entire universe.

I want you to take a moment and realize that what the whole universe is yearning for is you. Yes, you. All of creation is in anticipation of the day you wake up to the ability you have to be glorious and to gloriously influence everyone and everything everywhere you go.

In the original Greek of Romans 8:19, "glorious sons" is the word *huios*. It means *mature* sons. Scripture shows us very clearly in the book of Hebrews what it is to be mature in the things of God. A mature one in the kingdom is able to "recognize the difference between right and wrong" (Hebrews 5:14 NLT). Notice that a mature one does not decide for himself what is right or wrong but recognizes, according to the will and ways of God, what is good and what is evil—and then he chooses to do what is right. A mature son trusts in the love, goodness, wisdom, and truth of his heavenly Father and decides to obey his will and ways. A mature son knows the difference between right and wrong and chooses righteousness. He does not do this because it will earn him the love, favor, or blessing of his heavenly Father but because he knows he is loved, favored, blessed, and gets to co-labor with his Father to have a positive impact on the universe.

Every time you choose to honor and obey the will and ways of God, you are operating in heroic holiness, and it ripples throughout all of creation. We see this in Romans 5:18–19 (NLT):

> Adam's one sin brings condemnation for everyone, but Christ's one act of righteousness brings a right relationship with God and new life for everyone. Because one person disobeyed God, many became sinners. But because one other person obeyed God, many will made be made righteous.

Do you see it? When Adam chose to disobey, it was not just he who became unrighteous. Rather, it allowed unrighteousness to enter the earth and affect everyone. When Jesus chose to obey, it was not he who became righteous (he already was); rather, it made righteousness available to all. Adam was a son. Jesus is the Son. Decisions the sons of God make have the power to affect all of creation.

In Christ, you are restored to the fullness of relationship with your heavenly Father. You are a son of God. That means you are powerful. You have the ability to operate in heroic holiness and make a real difference in the world every time you choose righteousness.

The choices you make ripple throughout all creation. Your decisions not only affect your life, but they also affect the whole wide world. Choose sin and darkness, and sin and darkness enter the world. But, and this is a *huge* but, choose righteousness, and righteousness ripples throughout the earth. Choose love, patience, faithfulness, joy, mercy, kindness, or forgiveness, and they are released out into all of creation.

The powerful thing about heroic holiness is that it gives you a worldwide ministry. You don't need a TV show on the top Christian networks to reach the world with the power of Christ. You don't even need a best-selling book or a crusade. You simply need to operate in heroic holiness. Every time you do, you affect all of creation.

When you understand the blessing of heroic holiness, it changes everything. It is no longer a burden to resist the enemy and overcome temptation. It is an opportunity. When you choose not to give in to that temptation, you are being a glorious son and are gloriously influencing all of creation.

DECREES

I Decree That:

1. I am a mature son of God.
2. I recognize the difference between right and wrong and sin and virtue. In all things, at all times, I choose to obey the will and ways of my Father and to be a blessing to all creation.
3. I have the power in Christ to be a difference-maker on the earth.
4. When the enemy tries to tempt me, I choose to see it as an opportunity to operate in heroic holiness.
5. I am the very righteousness of God in Christ.
6. I submit no part of myself to wickedness but submit to the leading, encouragement, and empowerment of the Holy Spirit of God.
7. I am an instrument of righteousness.
8. By God's grace, I am saved, made righteous, and well able to deny all ungodliness and worldly lusts. I choose to live righteously and in a godly manner.
9. I abide in Christ, and he abides in me. I walk with the Holy Spirit of God. I am filled all in all with the Holy Spirit of God. I am not conformed to the desires of this world. I positively transform the world around me with every godly decision I make, bearing good fruit everywhere I go.
10. God has blessed me with heroic holiness.

Decrees based on the following Scriptures: Romans 8:19; Hebrews 5:14; 2 Corinthians 5:21; Romans 6:13–14; Titus 2:11–12; John 15:4; Galatians 5:16; Romans 12:2

ACTIVATION

The next time you are tempted in an area where you have wrestled, realize the temptation is not a burden that must be overcome. Temptation is an opportunity for you to operate in heroic holiness and arise as the glorious son that you are. Declare that you are a victorious champion of Christ on the earth. Realize that you are taking territory for the kingdom and releasing righteousness throughout all of creation. Way to go!

_____

_____

_____

_____

_____

_____

_____

_____

_____

_____

ABOUT THE AUTHOR

In November of 2002, Robert Hotchkin was splitting wood in the mountains of Montana when he was radically saved and forever changed by the first of many encounters with the love of Jesus. He went from being a mocker and persecutor of Christians to a passionate lover of Christ. That passion for the Lord marks his ministry, and it is truly contagious.

Robert is the apostolic leader of Men on the Frontlines and serves as one of the core leaders of Patricia King Ministries. He hosts the weekly *Heroes Arise* broadcast, co-hosts the show *Propel* with Patricia King, and is a regular guest and host of the shows *Everlasting Love* and *Supernatural Life* on GodTV. He also travels the world, ministering with strong faith and releasing revelation, prophetic decrees, healings, miracles, and the love of God. People have been healed, refreshed, set free, and empowered through his life.

Robert's preaching, teaching, and ministry inspire believers to grab hold of their restored relationship with the Father through the finished work of the cross and walk the earth as kingdom agents of impact.

Robert and his wife live in Scottsdale, Arizona. Connect with him online and through social media so that he can continue to pour into you:

Websites:	RobertHotchkin.com
	MenontheFrontlines.com
Facebook:	@OfficialRobertHotchkin
Twitter:	@RobertHotchkin
Instagram:	Robert Hotchkin
YouTube:	Robert Hotchkin Channel